GRUNDY'S TAX HAVENS:
A WORLD SURVEY

AUSTRALIA AND NEW ZEALAND
The Law Book Company Ltd.
Sydney : Melbourne : Perth

CANADA AND U.S.A.
The Carswell Company Ltd.
Agincourt, Ontario

INDIA
N.M. Tripathi Private Ltd.
Bombay
and
Eastern Law House Private Ltd.
Calcutta and Delhi
M.P.P. House
Bangalore

ISRAEL
Steimatzky's Agency Ltd.
Jerusalem : Tel Aviv : Haifa

MALAYSIA : SINGAPORE : BRUNEI
Malayan Law Journal (Pte.) Ltd.
Singapore

GRUNDY'S
TAX HAVENS:
A WORLD SURVEY

Fifth Edition

By

Milton Grundy, M.A. (Cantab)
of the Inner Temple and Gray's Inn, Barrister

LONDON
SWEET & MAXWELL
1987

First Edition
Etablissement Général des Instituts Financiers   1969

Second Edition
Sweet & Maxwell Limited: Matthew Bender & Co.   1972

Third Edition
The Bodley Head Limited & H.F.L.
    (Publishers Limited)   1974

Fourth Edition
Sweet & Maxwell Limited   1983
    Reprinted   1984

Fifth Edition
Sweet & Maxwell Limited   1987

Published by Sweet & Maxwell Limited
11 New Fetter Lane, London
Computerset by Promenade Graphics Limited
Cheltenham, Gloucestershire
Printed in Scotland

British Library Cataloguing in Publication Data
Grundy, Milton
    Grundy's tax havens: a world survey.—
    5th ed.
    1. Tax havens
    I. Title
    336.2'06   K4464.5

    ISBN 0–421–37900–6

Contents

Introduction

For its fifth edition, this book has been entirely rewritten. The format of previous editions was set by the first edition in 1969. I invited contributors from 14 tax havens to write a chapter, and the texts of their chapters (with a little diplomatic editing) formed the text of the book. One consequence of the huge growth of the offshore industry in the last 20 years is the growth in the number of jurisdictions with which the international tax planner is expected to be familiar. By the last edition, the number of territories had risen to 19. This edition covers 24, and even then I have had to leave out Andorra, Bahrain, Costa Rica, Djibouti, Grenada, Montserrat, Nevis, St. Vincent, Seychelles, Singapore, South Africa, Swaziland, and the U.S. Virgin Islands.

One solution to this problem would have been to allow the book to grow to a size when it could not be fitted into the average briefcase. As the reader will see, I have adopted the opposite solution—putting myself in the shoes of the reader, and asking myself just what kind of information he needs to have and limiting myself to that. With a few exceptions—with which few readers need concern themselves— the jurisdictions I have omitted merely duplicate facilities available in one or other of the territories I have included. The reader does not need to know, about any jurisdiction, the stamp duty payable on a resolution to change a company's name. Indeed, he does not need to know anything about the nuts and bolts of establishing trusts, companies and other entities. These are best left to the practitioner in the jurisdiction concerned. What the reader does need to know is whether there is a jurisdiction which will provide a likely answer to the problem in hand, and I have tried in this edition not to clutter up the pages with information which does not bear upon this question. I have given some indication in the text of the cost of, *e.g.* forming and maintaining a company in the various jurisdictions described. I have used the U.S. dollar as a common currency. While I hope this information will be useful, I do not want to exaggerate its importance: in a particular case, the actual cost will be affected by such factors as the number of nominee shareholders and directors required, the size of the share capital, safe custody of any bearer shares, the quorum for directors' and shareholders' meetings, any need for notarisation, and above all by the volume and complexity of the company's operations and the accounting consequences of its transactions. But if the aggregate of these costs amounts to a significant percentage of the expected profit, the venture is probably too small to warrant an offshore location. The old saying, that if you have to ask how much it will cost you can't afford it, applies with particular force to tax haven transactions.

I am grateful to my contributors, who enabled me to assemble in earlier editions information not readily available elsewhere. But by now, banks and trust companies in all the tax havens have produced a deluge of printed matter, and anyone can compile a huge dossier of information without any assistance from me. Where I hope the reader will find that I have been of some assistance is in reducing that information to its essentials.

An inevitable drawback in the old format of this book was that each chapter became, in the nicest possible way, a piece of propaganda for that jurisdiction. In this edition, I have tried to take a dispassionate view of the offshore world as a whole, and I have felt at liberty to express my opinions and preferences, even where these do not (and in many cases they do not) coincide with those of my esteemed colleagues in the jurisdictions of which I write. The reader may feel at liberty to disagree with them also. Necessarily, my observations are highly impressionistic. But I think that I have by now had—one way or another—experience of most kinds of offshore operations in most of these jurisdictions, and the opinions I express are a condensation of this experience.

I should like to express my gratitude to my pupil Philip Baker for his help with the writing of this book and to my colleague Edo de Vries for reading the text in typescript. I should also like to express my gratitude to the members of my advisory panel, listed below, who have very generously given time to reading the respective chapters in typescript and drawing my attention to the (now corrected) mistakes. The opinions and preferences, not to say prejudices and other shortcomings, are of course mine and not theirs.

I am indebted to readers and reviewers who have drawn my attention to shortcomings of earlier editions, and I should welcome suggestions for improvements to be made to the next.

Milton Grundy

Gray's Inn
London W.C.1.

May 31st, 1987

Advisory Panel

ANGUILLA

I. D. Mitchell,
Chambers,
P.O. Box 174,
The Valley,
Anguilla,
West Indies

ANTIGUA

William Cooper,
Antigua Management & Trust Ltd.,
P.O. Box 649,
McKinnons,
St. John's,
Antigua

BAHAMAS

Denis Catt,
The International Trust Group Ltd.,
P.O. Box N7767,
Bank Lane,
Nassau,
Bahamas

BARBADOS

Robert J. Bourque,
Robert J. Bourque & Co.,
135 Roebuck Street,
P.O. Box 806E,
Bridgetown,
Barbados

BERMUDA

The Bank of N. T. Butterfield, & Son
    Ltd.,
P.O. Box HM 195,
65 Front Street,
Hamilton 5,
Bermuda

BRITISH VIRGIN ISLANDS	Roger A. Dawes, International Trust Co. BVI Ltd., P.O. Box 659, Columbus Centre Bldg., Road Town, Tortola, British Virgin Islands
CAYMAN ISLANDS	Peter Stradling, RoyWest Trust Corporation (Cayman) Ltd., P.O. Box 707, West Bay Road, Grand Cayman, Cayman Islands
CHANNEL ISLANDS	David Singleton, Tortola Services Ltd., P.O. Box 129, St. Helier, Jersey, Channel Islands
COOK ISLANDS	Trevor Clarke, Clarkes, P.O. Box 144, Rarotonga, Cook Islands
CYPRUS	Chrysses Demetriades, Chrysses Demetriades & Co., P.O. Box 132, Fortuna Court/Block B, 284 Arch. Makarios III Av., Limassol, Cyprus

GIBRALTAR
Louis Triay,
Minster Management Services Ltd.,
31 Cannon Lane,
Gibraltar

HONG KONG
Peter Edwards,
Hamthor Ltd.,
11th Floor,
Alexandra House,
15–20 Chater Road,
Hong Kong

ISLE OF MAN
Charles Cain,
Charles Cain & Co.,
36 Finch Road,
Douglas,
Isle of Man

LIBERIA
Patrick L. Farrell,
Liberian Corporation Services Inc.,
Reston International Center,
Reston,
Virginia 22091,
U.S.A.

LIECHTENSTEIN
Dr. Guido Meier,
Algemeines Treuunternehmen,
P.O. Box 83,
FL–9490,
Vaduz,
Leichtenstein

LUXEMBOURG
E. Schmit,
Fiduciaire Générale de Luxembourg,
21 rue Vlesener,
Luxembourg

NAURU

M. N. Khushu,
Nauru Agency Corporation,
P.O. Box 300,
Nauru,
Central Pacific

NETHERLANDS
ANTILLES

Wil Kleinveld,
"Atruka" International Trust
(Curacao) NV.,
P.O. Box 523,
de Ruyterkade 51,
Curacao,
Netherlands Antilles

PANAMA

Norlando L. Pelyhe,
International Management and Trust
    Corpn.,
Apartado 7440,
Panama 5,
R de P

SWITZERLAND

Anthony J. Whitehouse,
RoyWest Trust Corporation S.A.,
Lausanne,
41 Avenue d'Ouchy,
Case Postale 110,
1000 Lausanne 13,
Switzerland

TURKS & CAICOS
ISLANDS

Seymour Gorman,
Incolex,
West Wing, Barclays Bank Building,
    PMB 9,
Grand Turk,
Turks & Caicos Islands,
B.W.I.

VANUATU

Toby A.S. Campbell,
Investors' Trust Ltd.,
P.O. Box 211,
Port Vila,
Vanuatu,
S.W. Pacific

Reference Maps

CHANNEL ISLANDS   **LONDON**
ISLE OF MAN   **UNITED KINGDOM**

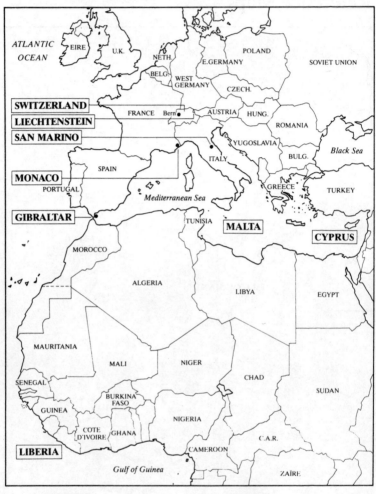

CYPRUS   **MALTA**
GIBRALTAR   **MONACO**
LIBERIA   **SAN MARINO**
LIECHTENSTEIN **SWITZERLAND**

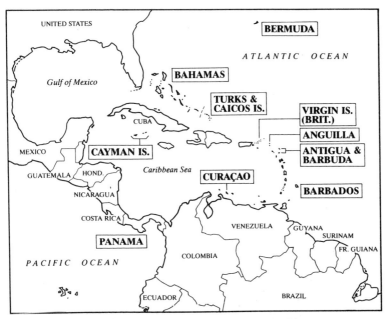

ANGUILLA	**CAYMAN IS.**
ANTIGUA & BARBUDA	**CURAÇAO**
BAHAMAS	**PANAMA**
BARBADOS	**TURKS & CAICOS IS.**
BERMUDA	**VIRGIN IS. (BRIT.)**

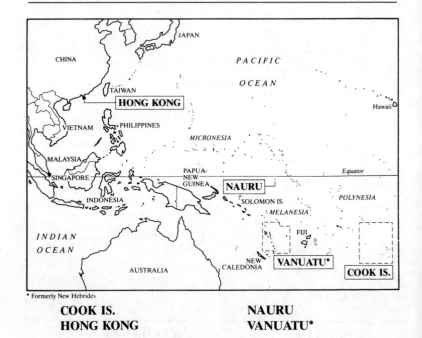

* Formerly New Hebrides

COOK IS.   **NAURU**
HONG KONG   **VANUATU***

Reference Table

COMPANIES (PRIVATE)	Anguilla	Antigua	Bahamas	Barbados	Bermuda	British Virgin Islands	Cayman Islands	Cook Islands	Cyprus	Gibraltar
Special kind of company required		IBC		IBC	Ex.	IBC		Ex.	INT.	Offshore
Bearer shares/warrants?	●	□	▲	●	●	□	●	□	●	▲
No par value shares?	●	□	●	□	●	□	●	□	●	●
One shareholder enough?	●	□	●	□	●	□	□	□	●	●
Ordinary shares freely redeemable?	●	□	●	□	□	□	●	▲	●	●
Corporate directors allowed?	□	□	□	□	●	□	□	□	□	□
More than one director required?	●	●	●	●	□	●	●	●	●	●
Local director/representative required?	●	□	●	●	□	□	●	□	●	●
Accounts required?	●	●	●	□	□	●	□	□	□	□
Accounts made public?	●	●	●	▲	●	●	●	●	▲	●
Are there optional endings for the corporate name?	●	□	●	□	●	□	●	□	●	●
Ultra vires rule?	□	●	□	●	□	●	□	●	□	□
Licence required for banks?	□	□	□	□	N.A.	N.A.	□	□	□	□
Licence required for insurance company?	□	□	□	□	□	●	□	□	□	□
Licence required for trust company?	●	□	□	□	N.A.	●	□	N.A.	●	●
Foreign income tax-free?	□	□	□	●	□	□	□	□	●	▲
Foreign income subject to low tax?	N.A.	N.A.	N.A.	□	N.A.	N.A.	N.A.	N.A.	□	□
Guarantee against future taxes?	●	□	●	▲	□	●	●	□	●	●
TRUSTS										
Foreign income and beneficiaries tax free?	□	□	□	□	□	□	□	□	□	□
Accumulation throughout perpetuity period?	□	□	□	□	□	□	□	□	□	□

KEY:-

IBC = International Business Company/Corporation
Ex. = Exempt
Non-Ex. = Non-Exempt
R = Resident
Non-R = Non-Resident

Corpn. T. = Corporation Tax Company
INT. = International Company
□ = yes
● = no
▲ = yes in some circumstances

Gibraltar	Guernsey	Hong Kong	Isle of Man	Jersey		Liberia	Liechtenstein	Luxembourg	Nauru	Netherlands	Netherlands Antilles	Panama
Ex.	Corpn. T.		Non-R	Ex.	Corpn. T.	Non-R	Anstalt (without shares)	S.A.	Holding Corpn.	B.V.	N.V.	S.A.
▲	●	●	□	□	●	□	□	□	□	●	□	□
●	●	●	●	●	●	□	N.A.	□	●	●	●	□
●	●	●	●	●	●	□	□	●	□	□	□	□
●	●	●	●	●	●	□	N.A.	□	□	□	□	□
□	□	▲	●	●	□	□	□	□	□	□	□	●
●	●	□	□	□	●	▲	●	□	●	●	●	□
●	●	□	●	□	●	□	□	●	□	●	□	□
□	□	□	□	□	□	□	▲	□	□	▲	□	●
●	●	●	●	●	●	●	●	□	●	▲	▲	●
●	●	●	●	●	●	□	□	●	□	●	●	□
□	□	□	▲	▲	□	●	●	●	●	●	●	▲
□	□	□	□	N.A.	□	N.A.	N.A.	□	□	□	□	□
□	□	□	□	□	▲	N.A.	N.A.	□	□	●	□	□
●	●	●	●	●	▲	□	N.A.	N.A.	□	□	□	□
□	□	□	□	□	□	□	□	□	□	▲	▲	□
N.A.	N.A.	N.A.	N.A.	N.A.	N.A.	N.A.	N.A.	N.A.	N.A.	●	□	N.A.
□	●	●	●	●	●	●	●	●	●	●	□	●
□	□	□	□	□	□	N.A.	□	N.A.	□	N.A.	N.A.	N.A.
□	□	●	□	□	□	N.A.	□	N.A.	□	N.A.	N.A.	N.A.

COMPANIES (PRIVATE)	Switzerland	Turks and Caicos		United Kingdom	Vanuatu
Special kind of company required	S.A.	Ex.	Non-R	Non-R	Ex.
Bearer shares/warrants?	□	□	□	□	□
No par value shares?	●	□	□	●	□
One shareholder enough?	●	□	□	●	●
Ordinary shares freely redeemable?	●	□	●	□	●
Corporate directors allowed?	●	□	□	□	□
More than one director required?	●	●	●	●	●
Local director/representative required?	□	□	●	●	□
Accounts required?	□	□	□	□	●
Accounts made public?	▲	●	●	□	●
Are there optional endings for the corporate name?	●	□	●	●	●
Ultra vires rule?	□	●	□	□	▲
Licence required for banks?	□	□	□	●	□
Licence required for insurance company?	□	N.A.	N.A.	●	□
Licence required for trust company?	●	●	●	●	□
Foreign income tax-free?	●	□	□	□	□
Foreign income subject to low tax?	▲	N.A.	N.A.	N.A.	N.A.
Guarantee against future taxes?	●	□	●	●	●
TRUSTS					
Foreign income and beneficiaries tax free?	□	□	□	▲	□
Accumulation throughout perpetuity period?	N.A.	□	□	●	●

KEY:-

IBC = International Business Company/Corporation
Ex. = Exempt
Non-Ex. = Non-Exempt
R = Resident
Non-R = Non-Resident
Corpn. T. = Corporation Tax Company
INT. = International Company
□ = yes
● = no
▲ = yes in some circumstances

Anguilla

The extraordinary growth of tax haven business is well illustrated by the story of Anguilla. When the third edition of this book was published there were no companies registered there. Now there are some 2,500.

It is a small island 150 miles east of Puerto Rico, visible from (and generally reached via) the Island of St. Maarten—the Dutch part of which is one of the territories which make up the Netherlands Antilles (q.v.). Apart from a small and rather up-market tourist industry, it has little economic activity, and fees from offshore companies form a significant part of government revenue. The island freed itself, in faintly comic circumstances, from an association with the former British colonies of St. Kitts and Nevis, and it reverted to colonial status in 1971. In 1976, it suspended exchange control; in 1977 it suspended income tax and abolished death duties. The stage was set for its development as a tax haven.

In the early days, the Colony acquired an unfortunate reputation as a home for phoney banks, but such abuses are a thing of the past: Government now enforces with due discrimination a system of "A" and "B" licences for banks and trust companies (trust companies, at least, with the word "trust" in their name), similar to that of the Bahamas. Anguilla's political horizon seems unclouded, and it appears to have escaped associations with narcotics and fraud and suchlike endemic misfortunes of unsophisticated territories which encourage their use as a base for sophisticated international business. For the client who is looking for an out-of-the-way place to incorporate a zero-tax company, Anguilla has a good deal to recommend it: costs are low; the companies registry is still small enough to present few problems to the registration of an acceptable name; the Island is an agreeable place to visit, and, once one has found out where it is, not difficult to get to from Europe or North America.

1

As in other British colonies, the law is derived from English law and English is the official language, and taxation and other domestic affairs are matters for the local legislature and not directed by the London Government. The local currency is the Eastern Caribbean Dollar. It is tied to the U.S. dollar, at the rate of E.C.$2.70 to U.S.$1.00. As in England, the law imposes a duty of confidentiality on lawyers, accountants and bankers. Like some other jurisdictions, Anguilla also has a Confidential Relationships Ordinance which makes breach of confidentiality a criminal offence.

The law relating to companies is essentially that of the United Kingdom before 1948. So—the word "Limited" (or "Ltd.") must appear at the end of the name; private companies do not file accounts but cannot have bearer shares; a local office is required but no local directors; shares of no par value are not permitted; the identity of shareholders and directors is public knowledge, but the registered shareholders may be nominees for the beneficial owners.

The fee for registering a company depends on its nominal capital, any share premium being left out of account. The practice is to form companies with a capital of E.C.$10,000 (U.S.$3,700), on which the registration fee is E.C.$500 (U.S.$185). The first E.C.$90,000 of any excess is charged at the rate of E.C.$100 per ten thousand and the rest at E.C.$50 per ten thousand.

Companies in Anguilla are formed by Company Formation Agents, of which there are presently six. It is possible to manage companies in the Colony, but its support services— in the way of banks, accounting firms, investment managers and so on—are few, and the true management and control of Anguillan companies is generally exercised elsewhere. It is possible in theory to establish partnerships, trusts, unit trusts and public companies there, but for the same reasons the client will generally look elsewhere for a base for such activities.

Antigua

Antigua merits a brief mention in this book, if only because its present facilities for the establishment of International Business Corporations are of fairly recent origin and not very widely known.

It is one of the larger islands of the Antilles chain, lying north of Barbados and south of the Virgin Islands. It has beaches and golf courses and a picturesque harbour with restored early 19th century buildings; it attracts a large number of tourists, especially in the winter months, and is well served by airlines from the United Kingdom and United States. It is a member of the British Commonwealth, and its language is English.

Antigua introduced provisions for the establishment of International Business Companies in the late Sixties, with a law in a form similar to that enacted in Jamaica (which has since repealed it), Barbados (which retains it with some modifications) and Grenada (which retains it in its original form). This was replaced in 1982 by the present International Business Corporations Act, which is an altogether more elaborate, American-style enactment, which provides for complete tax exemption for companies doing international business of whatever kind. The identity of the registered shareholders of an I.B.C. may be ascertained by examination of the Register, though nominee shareholders are permitted. An I.B.C. may have bearer shares or shares of no par value. It is not necessary to have more than one shareholder but the incorporator must be a licensed trust company or a member of the Bar. The company is free to redeem its ordinary shares. There is no minimum number of directors, nor (except in the case of a banking, trust or insurance company) any requirement for a director resident in Antigua, and corporate directors are permitted, but the company must have a resident agent in Antigua for service of process, and the annual meeting of shareholders (which may be held by proxy) must be held in Antigua. An I.B.C. is not required (unless it is engaged in banking, trust business or insurance) to keep or file accounts. The name of a company must include the word "Limited," "Corporation" or "Incorporated" in its full or abbreviated form, but may alternatively include a word or abbreviation used in another country to indicate that the liability of the shareholders of a body corporate is limited. The *ultra vires* rule does not apply to an I.B.C. The Act contains provisions for re-domiciliation.

A licence is required if a company is to carry on business as a bank or insurance company or trust company. An I.B.C. is exempt from taxes of all kinds in Antigua, and the Act provides for this exemption to continue in effect for a period of twenty years from the date of incorporation of the company. There is an initial and annual government fee of U.S.$250 (or U.S.$2,500 for companies licensed to carry on insurance or trust business and U.S.$5,000 for a bank).

Bahamas

The Commonwealth of the Bahamas is the true universal tax haven. It has companies and trusts in large numbers; there is a wide choice of lawyers, accountants and banks; it has a shipping registry and a free port; it hosts a huge amount of Eurodollar business; it offers facilities for captive and other insurance, unit trusts and mutual funds; most importantly, perhaps, its climate, beaches, sailing, golf, properties, restaurants and communications make it an attractive home for senior personnel. True, it is not as efficient as Hong Kong, nor as sophisticated as Switzerland, as classy as Bermuda or as cheap as Panama. But in whatever offshore activity the client wishes to engage, the chances are he can achieve it here, and the adviser who is new to the world of tax havens would do well to concentrate his energies on acquiring a detailed knowledge of the facilities offered by the Bahamas.

Nassau is the capital, on the Island of New Providence. This is the most populated, but not the largest, of some 700 islands in an archipelago stretching from Florida south-east towards Haiti. The facilities for international business are sited here—and to some extent in the duty-free zone on the island of Grand Bahama. Casinos, shops on Bay Street in the city centre and large hotels on the nearby beaches cater for cruise ship passengers and the demands of mass tourism. But there are also the large houses, yachts and executive jets, which confirm the image of the Bahamas as the millionaire's playground. The country as a whole, while prosperous by Third World—and indeed Caribbean—standards, has a discernible degree of social stress, which has alienated some foreign clients, but it has never fallen prey to racial conflict or civil disorder, and, while the business community has complained—not without justification—about government policy on the grant of work permits to expatriates, this seems to be a general feature of life in the Caribbean, and it has to

5

be said that the governments of each party have scrupulously respected the interests of foreign investors and clients of the offshore facilities.

The Bahamas is an independent country, a member of the British Commonwealth with a Westminster-style government. It has many remnants of a colonial past. Its law is based on the law of England and its ultimate court of appeal is the Privy Council in London. But New Providence is only 35 minutes flying time from Miami, and the country is very much a client state of the United States. The Bahamian dollar (B.$) is on par with the U.S. dollar; there is a high degree of co-operation with Washington in such matters as immigration and defence; the Bahamian Government has entered into a mutual assistance treaty with the U.S. Government, providing the Americans with access to information relating to the narcotics trade and other criminal activities. A Bahamian company is not the right vehicle for trading arms with Iran or selling computers to the Soviet Union. Nevertheless, Washington appears to recognise that the Bahamas serves to channel business and investment into the United States—the country having the use to the United States which Jersey has to Britain or Hong Kong to China, and has never pressed for any change in its tax haven status.

The Bahamas imposes no taxes on income, capital, capital gains or (except for a probate duty on the inheritance of local land) death. Unlike Bermuda, while there are ownership and work permit controls on foreigners doing business in the Bahamas the country has not sought to confine business in local hands, and the foreigner, who is at liberty to form a Bahamian company or partnership to do any kind of lawful offshore business, may well be welcomed also as an onshore investor. Though its company and trust laws are not so sophisticated as those of the Cayman Islands, the country is much larger and more populous, and it basically offers what Cayman and Bermuda also offer—a totally tax-free environment for international business.

A company in the Bahamas may be limited by shares or by guarantee, or unlimited; the company limited by shares is the vehicle usually chosen for international business. The minimum number of shareholders is five. Bearer shares can only be issued with the prior permission of the Central Bank, which is not easily obtained. Shares must have a par value. Ordinary shares cannot be redeemed or bought into treasury without the consent of the Court. Mutual funds sometimes overcome this difficulty by the use of companies limited by guarantee. The name of the company must end with the word *limited*. Although the abbreviation *Ltd.* is commonly used in commerce it is not authorised by the statute. The practice is to appoint a minimum number of two directors; corporate directors may be appointed. It is not necessary for a company to have a director resident in the Bahamas. The company is not required to keep or file accounts.

Banking, insurance, and trust business require licences. These fees are off-set against the company's registration fees. A system for licences ("A" onshore and "B" offshore) has been in operation since the mid 60s and is administered under the authority of the Minister for Finance, who will given a sympathetic ear to applicants with appropriate qualifications and credentials. For a general offshore licence the annual fee is $10,000; for a limited licence $3,000. Trusts in the Bahamas follow the English pattern (but without any limitation on the period for which income can be accumulated). There are large and well-established trust companies in Nassau, and numerous and large trust funds are administered there.

On the incorporation of a company, there are registration fees to pay to Government, which depend to some extent on the size of the authorised capital. The total cost of forming a small company will be in the region of $1,500. Maintenance costs are on the high side: the charge for a registered office is U.S.$1,000 a year and to this must be added the other expenses and a further $1,000 annual fee payable to Government (reduced to U.S.$100 if 60 per cent. Bahamian owned).

Barbados

With a high rate of literacy and an over-dependence on tourism, it is hardly surprising that the Government of Barbados should actively support, among other viable economic activities, the small but growing offshore industry. Barbados came into this field later than the Bahamas and the Netherlands Antilles; it is not a zero-tax jurisdiction and could therefore hardly be expected to enjoy the huge success of the Cayman Islands; but it has pursued this business with more determination than Jamaica, and more success than Antigua, Grenada or Montserrat.

Barbados is an independent country within the British Commonwealth. It has inherited the English law and language and is perhaps the most "British" of the Caribbean territories mentioned in this book. Access by air is easy, staying there is agreeable—with none of the sense of living in a tourist ghetto which visitors can feel on other Caribbean islands, and good professional and advisory services are available. The long-established facility which Barbados offers is the International Business Company. This is a company incorporated or resident in Barbados which does not trade in goods or services originating in Barbados. It may sell services originating in Barbados, so long as the services are rendered for or on account of persons resident outside the Caribbean Common Market area (which includes Barbados). If Barbadian residents have any interest in the equity or loan capital, this must not exceed 10 per cent. The company must elect not to receive credit in Barbados for foreign taxes on its foreign income. The company must be resident in Barbados but a company incorporated there will be deemed to be resident there. An I.B.C. is liable to tax on its profits at the rate of 2.5 per cent. No transfer tax is charged on transfers of shares in an I.B.C. or of its assets (other than real property situated in Barbados) to non-residents or another I.B.C. By special agreement with the Minister of Finance, a proportion (usually 35 per cent.) of salaries of specially qualified persons employed by an I.B.C. may be exempted from Barbadian income tax. No tax is levied on dividends or interest paid to non-residents or another I.B.C. An offshore bank pays tax at 2.5 per cent. (reducing to 1 per cent. depending on the level of profitability), but an exempt insurance company in Barbados, dealing with risks and premiums originating outside Barbados, is—no doubt so as to be competitive with Bermuda—exempt from tax altogether.

An investment company can also qualify as an I.B.C. It pays income tax at the rate of 2.5 per cent. on its first Bds.$10,000,000 (U.S.$5,000,000) of income per annum, 2 per cent. on the next 10,000,000, 1.5 per cent. on the next 10,000,000 and 1 per cent. on the residue.

To the cost of an I.B.C. must of course be added the cost of producing audited figures and agreeing profits with the Revenue authorities. There appear to be few situations where these costs are justified by benefits greater than those afforded by the use of a zero-tax company in another jurisdiction; but a Barbados company can be a U.S. Foreign Sales Corporation and there can be circumstances where it is desirable to pay tax, albeit at a low rate (involving *e.g.* Canada, Germany or the Netherlands), or where an I.B.C. can take advantage of the U.K. tax treaties with Switzerland (of 1954) and the Scandinavian countries, which were extended to Barbados.

The private company limited by shares is generally used for offshore activities. The company requires only one shareholder. The shares have no par value; the company may not issue bearer shares or bearer share certificates. The shares may be redeemed, so long as the company remains solvent. The name of the company must end in *limited*, *corporation* or *incorporated*, or *Ltd.*, *Corp.* or *Inc.* Only one director is required; there is no prohibition against corporate directors. Except for banks and exempt insurance companies it is not necessary to have a resident director. The company must keep accounts, and at present these are available for public inspection. The *ultra vires* rule does not apply. The fee payable to Government on incorporation is U.S.$390, but the main annual cost for an I.B.C. is, of course, the income tax to which it is liable. Licences are required for trust, banking and exempt insurance business. Banking and exempt insurance seem to be the growth areas of the offshore business in Barbados. It is Government policy to encourage such business and where the prospective enterprises are respectable, responsible and adequately capitalised, the licence will normally be granted.

Bermuda

It is the Belgravia of tax havens: it has established for itself—and to a great extent maintained—a position at the top end of the market. There are reasons for this, but they are not readily apparent.

Bermuda has the advantage—enjoyed also by the Bahamas and the Cayman Islands—of an historical freedom from direct taxes. Like them, it has agreed to help the United States Government in combatting crime. Like them, it has coral beaches and sunny skies, though it is much further north and considerably colder in winter. It, too, is part of the British Commonwealth, with English-derived laws and English as its language, being (like Cayman) a colony with internal self-government and the Privy Council in London as its final court of appeal. Its islands are not so close to the shores of the United States as are the Bahama Islands, but it hosts a U.S. naval base, and it is unthinkable that the Bermudians should bring to power a government to whose policies Washington was fundamentally opposed (not that they show any signs of wishing to do so). The population is some 60 per cent. black and 40 per cent. white. While the Bermudians claim—no doubt with justification—that there is a close equality between the communities in terms of power and wealth, the visitor has the impression that the communities mix and intermarry little, and the white community holds a dominating position in major economic activities—tourism, banking, insurance and the legal and accounting professions. But the visitor sees no sign of social stress. Bermuda is clean, well-kept and evidently prosperous.

The remarkable growth of Bermuda's offshore business after the Second World War may have owed something to its geographical position: not only are the flying times from London and New York shorter than those to the Bahamas, but in the days of the propeller-driven aeroplane it was a natural stopping-point between the two, and indeed it still commends itself as a meeting place for boards and committees including European and American members. Like a fashionable part of town, the status of its occupants attracts occupants of similar standing, and today Bermuda can fairly boast that no other offshore centre (unless it be Switzerland) has a comparable proportion of large corporations and rich families in its clientele. Bermuda has not won this position by being efficient or cheap, but by carefully excluding the undesirable clients. Although their ancestors made fortunes gun-running in the American civil war and rum-running during Prohibition, the present generation of bankers and professional practitioners have scrupulously avoided all involvement in activities which are to the slightest degree dubious, whatever personal profit they might promise, and it is to them, as much as to government regulation and supervision, that the Colony owes its untarnished and top-drawer image. By the same token, the intending client should arrive in Bermuda with credentials; the operator with a cheque book but no connections should look elsewhere.

This apart, the facilities offered by Bermuda do not differ essentially from those of other zero-tax jurisdictions—tax-free companies, settlements, pension funds, partnerships, unit trusts and mutual funds. The Bermudian offshore corporate vehicle is the Exempted Company, so called not because it is exempted from any existing tax (though it is entitled to exemption from any future taxes on profits, income, gains or capital assets until 2016), but because it is exempted from the requirements of the law which restrict non-Bermudian interests in local companies. Bermudian companies used to have to be incorporated by Private Act of the Legislature, but this procedure is now necessary only in special circumstances. Companies are generally formed by registration under the Companies Act 1981. Their powers are circumscribed by the *ultra vires* rule, but every power likely to be required is set out in a schedule to the Act and these are commonly adopted. Exempted Companies are not in general permitted to have any interest in local land or in local companies which are not Exempted Companies or to carry on business with Bermudians except in furtherance of their business overseas. The Registrar has power to refuse an undesirable name of a company and the name must end in "Limited' or "Ltd." The minimum share capital is $12,000. Greater share capital is required for insurance companies. Shares must be registered and have a par value. Three shareholders are required and the company must maintain a register of shareholders, open to inspection by the public, but the use of nominee shareholders is permitted. Exempted companies are not required to hold their board meetings in Bermuda, but must have at least two local directors, and every director must have a qualifying share (though he does not need to be the beneficial owner of it). An annual audit is required, and the auditor must be resident in Bermuda, though this requirement may be waived by all shareholders and all directors consent. The cost of compliance with these requirements must be taken into account in addition to the stamp duty of 0.25 per cent. on the authorised capital (subject to a maximum duty for insurance companies and their holding companies of $25,000) and an annual government fee of $1,200 ($2,250 for insurance companies, finance companies and mutual funds).

Exempted companies cannot carry on offshore banking or trust businesses. However, an Exempted Company may act as trustee of a named settlement or of settlements by members of a named family. Offshore insurance, by contrast, is encouraged. Over 6,000 Exempted Companies are now in existence, of which some 20 per cent. are registered to do insurance business. The concept of the offshore "captive" insurance company was first put into practice on a significant scale in Bermuda. Its practical as well as fiscal advantages have had a wide appeal. Adverse changes in the United Kingdom and the United States may lead to a diminution in business from these sources, but the Bermudians seem confident in the future of their insurance business, and, although the Cayman Islands and Guernsey—and, more recently, Barbados—have gained a small share of the market, the degree of expertise now available in Bermuda appears to ensure it retains the prime position in this field.

Settlements can be established in Bermuda, and many large funds are administered there. Stamp duty is charged at 0.1 per cent. on the value of the assets settled or subsequently added to the trust fund, together with a fixed fee of $250, subject to an overall maximum of $4,000. Bermuda requires its banks to be at least 60 per cent. locally owned; there are presently only three. The same rule is applied to companies carrying on the business of administering trusts, of which there are now fifteen.

Bermuda has for many years enjoyed the rather aristocratic reputation of being successful without trying too hard. Bermuda is for the Bermudians: a restrictive policy on immigration and business ownership has protected it from competition at home. But the competition is elsewhere, and there are signs that the present generation of bankers and professionals in Bermuda is anxious to meet it.

British Virgin Islands

What is known to the world as the British Virgin Islands (though it is officially "the Virgin Islands") is a group of sparsely populated, picturesque islands some 60 miles east of Puerto Rico. It is a British colony, with a legal system based on the common law, but its currency is the U.S. dollar (and was so even when it was part of the old Sterling Area). Its economy is closely linked to that of the United States and the U.S. Virgin Islands, and there is no exchange control. At their closest, the American islands are only a mile away; the Colony has no discernible anti-capitalist political activity, and the proximity of United States territory ensures that it will have none in the future. The airport on Beef Island takes only small aeroplanes; air communication is therefore via Antigua, San Juan or the U.S.V.I. The main island is Tortola—to which Beef Island is connected by a toll bridge, and the main town is Road Town. There are some banks, trust companies and firms of lawyers and accountants, the qualified personnel being mostly British, but their numbers are few and choice is limited.

From an international tax planning point of view, the outstanding attraction of the B.V.I. is the International Business Company (the "I.B.C."), made possible by the enactment of the International Business Companies Ordinance of 1984. It is still possible to form companies under the Companies Act of 1885 (as amended): such a company is required for local business and for banking and insurance, none of which an I.B.C. can presently undertake. A company formed under the 1885 Act is, if resident (*i.e.* managed and controlled in the B.V.I.), subject to tax at 15 per cent. on its world income, with credit for foreign tax on foreign income; it has full advantage of the tax treaties.

A company incorporated elsewhere but resident in the B.V.I. is subject to tax on its foreign income only to the extent that such income is remitted to the B.V.I.; since remittance is easily avoided, this limitation amounts in practice to an exemption, but such a company nevertheless obtains certain treaty benefits (see below).

Special provisions allow a resident company formed under the old law to pay tax on foreign income which is exempt from tax in its country of source (otherwise than by reason of treaty relief)—e.g. on interest on eurobonds—at the rate of only 1 per cent., but use of these provisions has been superseded by the I.B.C. Ordinance.

A resident company formed under the old law is subject to an annual fee by reference to the value of its non-B.V.I. assets. If the company is non-resident, it has no liability to tax on its income arising outside the Colony but obtains no treaty benefit. But the new law is more flexible and use of the old law—except for banking and insurance—has generally been superseded by the I.B.C.

The B.V.I. has income tax, but no taxes on capital, capital gains or death. Its tax system is essentially a simplified version of the U.K. statutes of 40 years ago, but, like the other British dependencies referred to in this book, no tax is in practice levied on the foreign income of trusts whose beneficiaries reside outside the colony. (For a fuller, though by now rather out-of-date, account of B.V.I. income tax, see McWelling Todman and Grundy, *Income Tax in the British Virgin Islands* Tortola Trust Corporation, P.O. Box 659, 1978).

The International Business Company has proved a remarkable success. The only real shortcoming of the 1984 Ordinance is that it requires the name of an I.B.C. to end in "Limited," "Corporation" or "Incorporated" or their abbreviations, (cf. the variety of endings permitted in Cayman, Liberia, Panama, and Turks and Caicos). Apart from this, the I.B.C. has some claim to be the best zero-tax company presently available. The legislation is lucid and brief, but confers enough statutory powers on a company to enable its memorandum and articles to be short. Only one shareholder is required; shares may be registered or bearer and have a par value or no par value; the articles and memorandum (including the provisions for share capital and name) are freely alterable; the objects may be shortly stated and there is no *ultra vires rule*; the identity of directors and shareholders is not public knowledge; there is no audit requirement; if shares are seized abroad, application may be made to the B.V.I. Court for such seizure to be disregarded; shares may be bought into treasury; corporate directors are permitted; no local director is required; meetings of directors and members' meetings need not be held in the B.V.I.; no A.G.M. or annual return is required; companies may merge; a company incorporated under the old law or in another jurisdiction can transfer to the I.B.C. register; an I.B.C. can re-domicile itself in another jurisdiction. An I.B.C. is exempt from income tax on its profits and on all dividends, interest, rents, royalties and other amounts paid to non-residents. No stamp duty is payable on transfers to or by an I.B.C., on any transactions relating to share capital or obligations or on the company's business transactions.

However, a company does not qualify as an I.B.C. if it carries on business with B.V.I. residents, owns an interest in B.V.I. land (other than a leasehold office) or accepts banking deposits or contracts of insurance. But it is not disqualified if in the B.V.I. it maintains a bank account, uses professional services, maintains accounting records, holds shareholders' or directors' meetings or holds local shares or other securities. It requires a registered office and a registered agent in the B.V.I. and has to pay a government fee of $300 on incorporation and $300 annually. (The fee is $1000 in each case if the authorised capital exceeds $50,000).

A banking or insurance company must be formed under the old Act. No licence is required for an insurance company (unless it writes local motor business), but for banks and financial institutions there is a licensing system, a minimum capital requirement and a Government fee—$10,000 a year for a general and $6,000 a year for a restricted licence. Trust companies require no licence.

Five tax treaties to which the United Kingdom was a party have been extended to the B.V.I.—those with Denmark (1956), Japan (1962), Norway (1956), Sweden (1954) and

Switzerland (1954). Later protocols, and the present (1977) treaty between the United Kingdom and Switzerland do not apply to the B.V.I. To take advantage of those treaties, a company must be resident in the B.V.I. for tax purposes. A company is deemed resident if more than half its directors are resident.

It is understood that Sweden has served notice to terminate its treaty and that Denmark does not always willingly permit its treaty to be applied.

Under a Bill now before the legislature, I.B.C.'s will be permitted to carry on banking business, subject to compliance with the provisions of the newly amended Banking Ordinance.

ANALYSIS OF BRITISH VIRGIN ISLANDS TAX TREATIES

COUNTRY OF SOURCE	RELIEVED IF TAXED IN B.V.I.					RELIEVED IN ALL CASES		
	INTEREST	ROYALTIES	DIVIDENDS		OTHER INCOME (not specifically covered in the treaty)	COMMER-CIAL & INDUSTRIAL PROFITS (no permanent establishment)	SHIPPING PROFITS	CAPITAL GAINS
			50% share-holding or more	less than 50%				
DENMARK	X	E(1)	E	5%	X	E	E	E
JAPAN	10%	10%(2)	10%	15%	X	E	E	E
NORWAY	X	E(2)	E	5%	X	E	E	X (3)
SWEDEN	E(4)	E	E(5)	E(5)	E	E(6)	E	E
SWITZERLAND	X	E(2)	X	X	X	E	E	E

Key:
E = exempt
X = no provision in the treaty

Notes: (1) does not apply if recipient owns 50% of payer
(2) does not apply to mining or similar royalties
(3) gains on the sale of patent rights are exempt
(4) there is no interest provision in the treaty—exemption arises from the "other income" article
(5) exempt from Swedish coupon tax
(6) does not apply to athletes & artistes

21

Cayman Islands

In the large expanse of the Caribbean Sea between Jamaica and Cuba are the three islands—one small and two very small—which make up the Cayman Islands. The Territory is a British Colony, with English-style laws, but a currency—the Cayman dollar—tied to the U.S. dollar (U.S.$1.20 = C.I.$1.00). There is no exchange control. George Town, its capital, invites comparisons with Nassau. Though altogether on a smaller scale, it too abounds with banks and trust companies and has international accounting firms and experienced lawyers; Caymanians, like Bahamians, have always been free of direct taxes and intend to remain so; in comparison with the Bahamas, the Cayman Islands has fewer amenities for expatriate staff, but the absence of any history of racial conflict, and the general prosperity and absence of unemployment which have resulted from the tremendous growth in the last 15 years of tourism and offshore business, give it a claim to a greater degree of political stability.

Like Nassau, George Town has attracted a good deal of offshore banking business. Cayman has a licensing system for banks (applying also to trust companies) which is an exact copy of that in force in the Bahamas; the licence fee for class B (offshore banks) is C.I.$9,000 (U.S.$10,800) for an unrestricted licence and C.I.$6,000 (U.S.$7,200) for a restricted licence.

In recent years, Cayman has also attracted some insurance and re-insurance business. The Insurance Law of 1979 provided the legal framework, with a similar system of class A licences (C.I.$5,000) (U.S.$6,000) and class B licences (C.I.$4,500) (U.S.$5,400). More importantly, there are now some individuals residing there who have underwriting expertise, and the Cayman Islands may be seriously considered as a viable alternative to Bermuda for captive and other offshore insurance companies.

An attempt on the part of the Cayman Government to attract shipping registration seems to have been less successful, but a number of successful investment funds have been established there without requiring any special legislation. Those intended to interest investors from the United Kingdom and elsewhere in the British Commonwealth take the form of English-style unit trusts; others are formed as companies—investments in them taking the form of preference shares with a low par value, as in the Channel Islands.

The ordinary company in the Cayman Islands is a satisfactory zero-tax vehicle, requiring only one shareholder. The Companies Law is modelled on the U.K. Act of 1948 and has a useful provision for striking off inactive companies without the necessity for liquidation. It provides also for Exempted Companies. These are companies which carry on business only outside the Cayman Islands. They pay higher Government fees (on incorporation, C.I.$850 plus 0.1 per cent. of the authorised capital in excess of C.I.$750,000 up to a maximum of C.I.$1,900 and an annual C.I.$475 plus 0.05 per cent. of excess capital up to a maximum of C.I.$1,300, as opposed to an initial C.I.$500 for the first C.I.$800,000 capital for an ordinary company, plus 0.05 per cent. of the excess up to C.I.$1,350 and an annual C.I.$250 plus 0.025 per cent. of the excess up to C.I.$650); in return they are exempted from some requirements of the Companies Law. They are not required to file annual returns, to keep registers of members, to hold annual general meetings or to include the word "limited" in their name. They may issue bearer shares and shares of no par value. They may also obtain a 20 year guaranteed exemption from tax. But they are not emancipated from the *ultra vires* rule, they have no general ability to reduce their share capital and cannot redomicile themselves.

For the establishment and administration of trusts, Cayman provides facilities similar to those of the Bahamas, with the addition of a facility for what the Trusts Law (Revised) terms an Exempted Trust. Four types of trust may be created under Cayman Islands law:

1. an ordinary trust;
2. an exempted trust;
3. a section 77 exempted trust;
4. a section 79 exempted trust.

These have the following features:

An ordinary trust may be created in any form permissible under English law (but without any restriction on the period during which income may be accumulated).

A trust may be registered as an exempted trust under Part V of the Trusts Law. This differs from an ordinary trust in three respects:

(i) The original trust instrument is lodged in a file kept by the Registrar of Trusts; the file is not open to public inspection, nor to inspection by anyone other than the trustees and persons expressly authorised by the trust instrument.

(ii) A registration fee of C.I.\$200 (U.S.\$240) and an annual fee of C.I.\$100 (U.S.\$120) are payable to the Registrar of Trusts.

(iii) The Governor of the Cayman Islands may give an undertaking, exempting for a period, not exceeding fifty years, the trust property and income from any taxes imposed in the future in the Cayman Islands. As a matter of practice the Governor does give such an undertaking.

A "section 77" exempted trust is one approved under section 77 of the Trusts Law 1967 in advance of being created. This differs from other exempted trusts in that the exemption from tax is given in advance. A further advantage of a section 77 trust is that it may have a perpetuity period of a specified number of years not exceeding one hundred.

A "section 79" exempted trust must contain at least some discretionary trust or power to appoint or apply capital or income to or for the benefit of the beneficiaries. It has the same features as a section 77 exempted trust, with two important differences:

   (i) It is not capable of being varied by the Court under Part IV of the Trusts Law

  (ii) No beneficiary has any right to enforce the trust, whether he has under the terms of the trust instrument a vested or contingent or other interest, or merely an expectancy as the object of a power or discretion. The trustees may be sued for breach of trust only by their successors as trustees or by the Registrar of Trusts. No beneficiary is entitled to any information, or to inspect or to copy documents, relating to the trust.

The practical importance of a section 79 trust is that it enables a settlor to confer benefits on children or on adult beneficiaries of unsound mind or weak personality or on individuals he thinks might turn out to be greedy or grasping, without giving them any right in law to apply to the Court or otherwise make nuisances of themselves in the event that the trustees decide not to exercise their discretion in their favour.

The recent Trusts (Foreign Element) Law is designed to ensure that the provisions of a trust instrument governed by Cayman Law shall prevail over any claims by heirs or others under the law of the settlor's domicil.

The Confidential Relationships (Preservation) Law makes breach of confidence a criminal offence. The Cayman Islands has had since 1984 an agreement with the United States for obtaining and providing information relating to narcotics offences and has agreed a more general legal mutual assistance treaty for the exchange of information in criminal matters. Specifically excluded from the treaty are any matters relating directly or indirectly to the imposition or collection of taxes. This treaty has yet to be ratified by the United States Senate.

Channel Islands

These are islands a few miles off the coast of France and some 70 miles from the United Kingdom. They are not constitutionally part of the United Kingdom, but remnants of the Duchy of Normandy, of which the Queen of England is presently the Duke, in succession to William the Conqueror. Although they have close political, economic, social (and gastronomic) ties with England, the Channel Islands are—importantly in our context—not part of the United Kingdom for tax purposes. They are not part of the EEC: they are part of the EEC customs union, but have no value added tax and are not required to adopt the community's fiscal policies.

They comprise four jurisdictions—Jersey, Guernsey, Alderney and Sark. Sark is the smallest of these. It has no income tax, but no facilities for forming companies and no serious facilities for offshore activities of any kind. Many people who ought to know better have persuaded themselves that they can have companies incorporated elsewhere "managed and controlled" in Sark, and not resident elsewhere, by having sea-sick directors on a day trip sign minutes on the quayside, and it appears that the tax authorities in the other islands will grant "corporation tax" status (see below) to companies whose registered directors have addresses in Sark; but it seems unlikely that such arrangements would survive serious challenge.

But Guernsey (whose taxes extend to Alderney) and Jersey are serious offshore centres, with a due compliment of lawyers, accountants, banks and trust companies. They are separate, and competitive, but offer basically the same facilities. Of the two, Jersey, with an estimated 25,000 companies, is the busier and more successful; but Guernsey has an estimated 10,000 companies, and has attracted some captive insurance business. What is said in the next three paragraphs about Jersey applies equally to Guernsey, except where otherwise stated.

A company which is "managed and controlled" in Jersey is resident there, and pays income tax at 20 per cent. on its world income. In Guernsey, however (but not in Jersey) express provision is made for a resident mutual fund or unit trust whose investors are non-residents to be treated itself as non-resident. The rules regarding residence follow those of the United Kingdom: in determining a company's residence, the Revenue authorities will look primarily at the place where the directors hold their meetings and "income" is calculated on U.K. principles. There is an old and not very extensive tax treaty with the United Kingdom, whose most useful provision is that exempting from U.K. tax the industrial or commercial profits of a Jersey resident who does not have a permanent establishment in the United Kingdom.

As in the United Kingdom, it is the residence and not the place of incorporation of a company which determines its general liability to tax. If a company is incorporated in Jersey but not resident there, its liability to Jersey tax is limited, like that of any other non-resident, to tax on income which arises within Jersey, other than bank interest. All companies pay an annual government fee of £100 a year; non-resident companies pay an additional fee of £500 a year, confusingly called "corporation tax." In practice a company will be recognised as a "corporation tax company" only if it is owned by non-residents and does not trade in Jersey.

The common law of Jersey derives from Norman customary law, but legislation follows English patterns and the law relating to business and corporate activity is mainly English in character, with the Privy Council as the final court of appeal. English is the language in common use, though French is still used in conveying property. The currency is the pound sterling.

Jersey's success as an offshore centre has strained its physical resources. Licences are required to establish a new business, to increase the space occupied by an existing business or to immigrate; these have become increasingly difficult to obtain. Consent is required for the issue of any shares, but few restrictions are in practice placed on the incorporation of local companies so long as its objects do not include anything which appears undesirable. A Jersey company must have a registered office in Jersey and must include the word "Limited" in its name. Only registered shares are permitted, and the register must be available for public inspection. Shares must have a par value, but that may be in any currency other than the Swiss franc. There must be at least three shareholders (seven in Guernsey), but nominee shareholdings are permitted. "Off-the-shelf" companies are not available. A company cannot redeem ordinary shares but this rule is commonly circumvented by mutual funds, whose "equity" is represented by participating preference shares with a derisory nominal value and a large premium. The law does not prescribe a minimum number of directors nor does it forbid corporate directors. No local director is required. A Guernsey company must have an auditor, but in Jersey companies need not be audited, though resident companies arc in practice audited since their tax liabilities have to be agreed with the Comptroller of Income Tax. Annual General Meetings must be held in Jersey. Particulars of shareholders (and in Guernsey of directors) are included in the company's annual returns, but the accounts of Jersey companies are not made public. A company cannot act outside the objects set out in its memorandum (*ultra vires*) and the objects cannot be altered after registration. Incorporation costs in Jersey start at £450 (U.S.$720); in Guernsey, at £650 (U.S.$1,040).

A large amount of trust business is done in both Guernsey and Jersey. The legal foundation for the trust in these jurisdictions is mysterious, but the courts have in practice applied the English rules of equity. Many of these have now been codified in Jersey (but not in Guernsey) in a statute—the Trusts (Jersey) Law 1984. The draftsman took the opportunity of adding some features not found in the law of England, permitting a perpetuity period of 100 years and imposing on the "directors" (an expression widely defined) of a corporate trustee a personal liability for any breach of trust committed by the company. By concession, no tax is charged on trust income arising outside Jersey or consisting of interest on local bank deposits, so long as no-one resident in Jersey has any actual or contingent interest in the trust, whether the income is distributed or accumulated. The establishment of trust companies is carefully regulated. A licence is required for a bank, and this will be granted, if at all, only to a bank of international standing.

Many open-ended investment funds have been established in each of these islands, either in corporate form or in the form of a unit trust. Government consent is required for any new issue of shares or units, and this is given cautiously. The income of the fund and distributions to investors are not subject to local tax, except in the hands of local residents. Captive insurance and re-insurance companies may be established but require permits; permits may also be granted for a wider range of insurance business, but the applicant must be entitled to carry on such business in an EEC member state.

The Cook Islands

They are everyone's dream Pacific islands, with lagoons and palm trees and visitors greeted at the airport with garlands of frangipani. But they are exceedingly remote from the world's principal financial centres, and even from Australia, they are, confusingly, on the other side of the International Date Line. Surprisingly, in the early Eighties they enacted some well-thought-out legislation, which has made the territory an attractive place for the establishment of offshore banks, offshore insurance companies and other zero-tax companies.

The territory is self-governing, but has close links with New Zealand. The islands use New Zealand currency. English is spoken, and the law, the legal system and government follow the English pattern.

Its zero-tax companies are formed under the International Companies Act 1981–82. Schedules to the Act provide standard forms of memorandum and articles, which may be adopted with or without modifications. If no modifications are required, the constitution of a company fits comfortably on to a single page. Only one subscriber is required, and he may be the nominee of the beneficial owner. There is no minimum capital requirement. Shares may be registered or in bearer form, and may but need not have a par value. They may be designated in any of the major currencies. The minimum number of directors is one and there is no requirement for a local director. It is, however, necessary to have a resident secretary, who must be an officer of a recognised trust company, though additional non-resident secretaries can be appointed. The registered office of the company must be at the office of a recognised trust company.

The Companies Register contains copies of the certificate of incorporation and of the memorandum and articles of association, particulars of the authorised capital, the address of the registered office and a memorandum of appointment or power of attorney authorising a local trust company to accept service of process and notices. It also lists the directors and secretaries, and if any local director is appointed, the company must lodge a memorandum stating his powers. While the Register shows the number of shares allotted, it contains no information as to the identity of the shareholders.

The Act contains provisions for redomiciliation. Both the memorandum and the articles may be changed by special resolution. The name of the company may be similarly changed, but must always end with one of the words *Corporation*, *Corp.*, *Incorporated*, *Inc.*, *Limited*, or *Ltd*. The company may purchase its own shares, but only out of earned surplus. The Act provides for bearer debentures, for the conversion of bearer debentures to registered debentures, for perpetual debentures and for the re-issue of redeemed debentures. It contains also a useful provision for the voting rights of shareholders to be suspended during such time as certain types of debenture are in issue.

A company must hold an annual general meeting but the shareholders may agree to meet outside the Cook Islands or even to dispense with a meeting and sign a resolution in writing. A brief annual return is required, but no accounts need to be lodged. The Act contains provision for the Registrar to strike off companies considered to be defunct. There is a guarantee against expropriation or compulsory acquisition of a company's assets except in accordance with due process of law, for a public purpose and upon payment of due compensation. Certain public offerings require a prospectus to be registered. There is no requirement that directors' meetings be held in the Cook Islands, and although the company must maintain proper books of account, audit is not generally required, nor group accounts, nor is there a requirement for the filing of accounts.

Companies formed under the International Companies Act enjoy a complete exemption from all forms of taxation in the Cook Islands, including withholding tax on dividends paid to non-residents. As is usual in high tax jurisdictions which make special provisions for exempt companies, the exemption is conditional upon the company entering into no business or other contractual arrangements with residents of the Cook Islands, though exceptions to this rule may be made in the interests of development of the Cook Islands themselves.

The government fees for international companies are on the high side, relative to the charges for comparable facilities elsewhere. The fee payable on incorporation is U.S.$ 1,000, and U.S.$500 is payable annually.

The Offshore Banking Act establishes a licensing system for offshore banking. For an unrestricted ("Class A") licence, the annual fee is U.S.$10,000, but a restricted ("Class B") licence can be obtained for as little as an annual U.S.$2,000. Tax on interest paid to depositors is specifically exempt, and the Act embodies provisions for bank secrecy. Companies holding banking licences require to be audited and to submit annual reports to the relevant government department.

A system of licensing offshore insurance companies was established by the Offshore Insurance Act. The Act contains similar provisions for audit, the lodging of an annual report and the protection of secrecy, together with minimum net asset requirements. The licence fee for the first year is U.S.$2,000 and U.S.$500 is payable annually.

Cyprus

Cyprus is a large island in the eastern Mediterranean, with a population of Greek and Turkish descent. It was formerly a British colony and retains a system of law which is mostly English. Since 1974, the northern part of the island has been under Turkish occupation; the legitimate government rules over the southern part, which is Greek-speaking, though English is widely used. This chapter deals with the southern part which is internationally recognised.

Cyprus offers facilities for trusts and partnerships, and for companies of various kinds—private and public and limited by shares or guarantee, as well as "hybrid" companies with guarantors and shareholders. But its distinguishing features, from a tax point of view, are two. First, it has limited facilities for zero-tax operations. The profits of shipping companies with ships registered in Cyprus are not taxed, nor are profits of partnerships of non-Cypriots or profits of branches of non-Cypriot companies managed and controlled elsewhere whose shareholders are non-Cypriot, so long as the partnership or branch is wholly engaged in offshore activities. A branch of a foreign bank conducting an offshore banking business (an "Offshore Banking Unit") pays an annual fee of U.S.$15,000, but is not subject to any local tax on its profits. A licence is required, and this is only granted to banks of international standing and their subsidiaries. No tax is levied on the income of trusts, where both the settlor and the beneficiaries are non-resident, and the trust income has a source outside Cyprus.

Second, and more importantly, non-resident aliens may form a company in Cyprus, which is managed and controlled there and accordingly resident there both for domestic and for treaty purposes, but which is liable to tax on its offshore income only at the rate of 4.25 per cent. Such an "offshore" company is not liable to capital gains tax (except on gains from immovable property situated in Cyprus) and no withholding or other tax is chargeable on its dividends. Shares in an offshore company are exempt from estate duty, and gains arising from the disposal of its shares are free of capital gains tax. In this field, the nearest rival to Cyprus is the Netherlands Antilles. Cyprus has the disadvantage here that "residence" for treaty purposes may be harder to prove: the Cyprus treaties adopt a "management and control" test, whereas incorporation in the Antilles prima facie qualifies a company as resident there for treaty purposes. But Cyprus has the advantage of having more treaty partners and amongst them practically all eastern European countries, and its low tax facilities for doing business with those countries are unrivalled. The effect of the tax treaties is set out in the table below. Foreign employees of an offshore company (or of an offshore partnership or branch) pay tax in Cyprus at a reduced rate—the highest bracket being 30 per cent. if their duties are performed in Cyprus, or 6 per cent. if their duties are performed elsewhere.

The private company limited by shares is the vehicle generally used for offshore activities. Its capital must be expressed in Cyprus Pounds (though the company may keep its books in any currency) and the minimum paid-up capital is CY.£1,000 (U.S.$2,100). Two shareholders are required, and nominees are permitted. Shares must be registered shares with a par value. Ordinary shares cannot be redeemed without the consent of a court. The company's name must end in "Limited."

The company may have a single director and corporate directors are permitted. There is no obligation that the directors reside in Cyprus, but offshore companies wishing to show that they are "managed and controlled" in Cyprus will normally have a preponderance of local residents on the board. Similarly, while the law does not require directors' meetings to be held in Cyprus, the company wishing to show residence in Cyprus will hold its board meetings there. The company must have a registered office in Cyprus. An Annual General Meeting must be held and annual audited accounts must be prepared and submitted to the authorities. Returns have to be made, showing the shareholders, the registered office and the directors: these are open to public inspection. The Central Bank of Cyprus will designate the company non-resident for exchange control purposes: it is thereupon exempt from all requirements of Cyprus exchange control, and may, if it wishes, operate a bank account abroad or an external bank account in Cyprus.

Offshore banking may be conducted by an offshore company, as an alternative to an Offshore Banking Unit; this may be advantageous where treaty benefits are sought. Offshore companies also function as captive or other insurance companies; to carry on any insurance business, government approval is required.

CYPRUS: TAX TREATIES

Country	Dividends[1]	Interest[2]	Royalties[3]	Business Profits[4]	Other Income[5]
BULGARIA	10%	10%	exempt[6]	Y	Y
CANADA	15%	15%	10%[7]	Y	Y[8]
CZECHOSLOVAKIA	10%	10%	5%	Y	Y
DENMARK	15% (10% if >25% shareholding)	10%	exempt	Y	Y
FRANCE	15% (10% if >10%)[10]	10%	exempt[9]	Y	Y
EAST GERMANY	exempt	no limit	exempt	Y	N
WEST GERMANY	15% (10% if >25%)[12]	10%	exempt[11]	Y	Y
GREECE	25%	10%	exempt[13]	Y	Y
HUNGARY	15% (5% if >25%)	10%	exempt	Y	Y
IRELAND	exempt	exempt	exempt[14]	Y	Y
ITALY	15%	10%	exempt	Y	Y
KUWAIT[15]	10%	10%	exempt[16]	Y	Y
NORWAY	5% (exempt if >50%)	not covered	exempt	Y	N
ROMANIA	10%	10%	exempt[17]	Y	Y
SWEDEN	5% (exempt if >50%)	not covered	exempt	Y	N
UNITED KINGDOM	15%[18] (exempt if >10%)	10%	exempt[19]	Y	Y[20]
UNITED STATES	15%	10%	exempt	Y	N
U.S.S.R.	exempt	exempt	exempt	Y	Y
YUGOSLAVIA[21]	10%	10%	10%	Y	Y

1. maximum withholding tax on payment of dividends to Cyprus
2. maximum withholding tax; N.B. interest on certain loans, (*e.g.* to Government) may qualify for exemption from withholding tax
3. maximum withholding tax
4. Y = business profits exempt if no permanent establishment
5. tax treaty contains an article exempting other income not specifically mentioned in the treaty from taxation in the country of source
6. 5% for patent royalties
7. copyright royalties exempt
8. can also be taxed in country of source; trust income subject to 15% maximum tax in the country of source
9. 5% for film royalties
10. includes repayment of the precompte
11. as footnote 9
12. or 27% if direct or indirect holding is 25% or above
13. as footnote 9
14. as footnote 9
15. not yet in force
16. as footnote 6
17. as footnote 6
18. includes tax credit
19. as footnote 9
20. does not apply to payments from trusts
21. not yet in force

Gibraltar

Gibraltar is a large rock with a small amount of surrounding land, on the north shore of the Straits of Gibraltar, which divide the western Mediterranean from the Atlantic Ocean. It is a British Colony with internal self government, and has been a British possession since 1704. It functioned as a fueling and repair depot for the British navy and had obvious strategic importance to the British Empire, but these functions have now passed, and the territory has been much in need of alternative economic activities.

Spain lays claim to the sovereignty of Gibraltar, and as a way to bring pressure on the British government to acknowledge its claim kept its frontier closed for many years. This inflicted further damage on the economy of the Colony. Gibraltarians speak Spanish as well as English; they have resolutely refused to be incorporated with Spain, and it is a policy of the British government not to make any changes to the constitution of Gibraltar which is contrary to the wishes of the population. The dispute has not been resolved, but its intensity has been much lowered, partly by the restoration of the democratic government in Spain, partly by the addition of Spain to the EEC, but most noticeably by the reopening of the frontier.

The Gibraltar government recognised the possible contribution which an offshore financial industry could make to the economy and enacted legislation to enable non-Gibraltarians to incorporate zero-tax companies in Gibraltar. The tax exemption of companies in the Channel Islands and the Isle of Man is based (as in the United Kingdom) on their being non-resident in the jurisdiction concerned. The freedom from tax in Gibraltar is on a different principle—that the company's exemption should not depend on its residence, but upon a certificate of exemption issued by the Financial Secretary. The legislative provisions are to be found in the well drafted, if inelegantly titled, Companies

(Taxation and Concessions) Ordinance 1983. This gives Gibraltar a considerable advantage over its more established competitors in the other British Islands. It is advantageous to the local economy that individuals resident in Gibraltar can, and commonly do, constitute the whole or majority of the board of directors of an exempt company. Meetings are held there and business is done there; an exempt company may have an office in Gibraltar, employ local staff and have an entry in the telephone directory, and still retain its exempt status. This is advantageous also to the client who requires an "on the ground" operation. It is not at all easy to find in Europe a location where a company can have an open physical presence but not be subject to local tax on its income or profits. Luxembourg and the Isle of Man (*q.v.*) offer this opportunity for certain business activities, but Gibraltar is the only place in Europe where international business of any kind may be conducted from a local office without any exposure to local tax.

The reopening of the frontier with Spain has had a dramatic effect on the economy of Gibraltar. This is immediately apparent by the number of visitors thronging Main Street. But it has a less visible component: foreigners living in southern Spain are coming to regard Gibraltar as the natural centre for the conduct and administration of their affairs; the exempt company has proved a popular vehicle for foreigners to hold real property in Spain; and clients and professional advisers in other parts of Europe are not so reluctant to take the journey to Gibraltar, now that it can be combined with a round of golf in Soto Grande or a drive up to Rhonda. The Gibraltar government maintains its firm support of the offshore industry, and there are even signs that the government in Madrid is coming to recognise that a tax haven on one's back door-step significantly facilitates foreign investment inflows, and is coming to see Gibraltar in the same light as London sees Jersey, Beijing sees Hong Kong and even Paris sees Monaco.

The rules that govern the operation of exempt companies are essentially designed to ensure that they are not a vehicle for the avoidance of tax by Gibraltarians or local business, and that they do not besmirch the name of Gibraltar by conducting undesirable activities. An exempt company must not, without specific approval, carry on a trade or business in Gibraltar, other than the buying, selling, holding, managing, rendering or promoting services, investments, property, choses in action and things situated outside Gibraltar. An exempt company must not keep a share register outside Gibraltar, and no Gibraltarians, or residents of Gibraltar may be beneficially interested in its shares, though they may hold such shares as trustees. When applying for an exemption certificate, a company must furnish to the Finance and Development Secretary the names of its directors, of the beneficial owners of its shares and of its auditors. Any bearer shares must be deposited with a bank to the order of persons approved by the Finance and Development Secretary. The company must also disclose the nature of its activities and its share structure. Transferees of shares in an exempt company must be approved by the Finance and Development Secretary. This information must be, and in practice is, treated by Government as confidential. An exemption certificate grants full exemption from income tax and estate duty and is valid for 25 years from the date of issue, provided that the annual tax or fee is paid and that the other requirements of legislation are complied with. Exempt companies are not liable to withholding tax on dividends.

While the degree of information disclosed is high for the establishment of an exempt company in Gibraltar—compared, let us say, with that required for the formation of an international business company in the British Virgin Islands, and the legislation is more restrictive in character than that found elsewhere, these features do not appear in practice to prove unduly irksome. There is no requirement in the Companies Ordinance for a private company to file a balance sheet, but an auditor must be appointed. Two shareholders are required, who may be nominees. Shares may be held by trustees, and changes in the beneficial interests in the trust do not require government approval. In practice, at least two directors are appointed; they can be of any nationality and reside anywhere in the world but their identity must be disclosed on the company's writing paper, circulars etc. An exempt company may express its share capital in any currency. The company must file notices relating to its registered address or any changes of its registered address, to its allotment of its shares, to its appointment of directors and secretary and to the creation by it of mortgages or charges. A return containing a list of all persons who on the 14th day after the first or only ordinary general meeting in a year are members of the company, and of all persons who have ceased to be members, must be filed once a year. Such annual return must state the registered address of the registered office and contain particulars of the share capital of the company, showing the shares allotted and the amounts called up on each share, particulars of all persons who are the directors of the company and the total amount of the indebtedness of the company in respect of all the mortgage and charges require to be registered. Shares of no par value are not permitted. Ordinary shares cannot be redeemed without the consent of the court. The company's name must end with "Limited."

The law of Gibraltar is based on English Law. The Privy Council in London is the final court of appeal. English is the official language and legal and commercial affairs are conducted in English. The currency is the Gibraltar Pound, which is on a par with the Pound Sterling. There were formerly some fears—which may or may not be well founded—that exchange control might be reintroduced in the United Kingdom and if this were to happen Gibraltar would be within the new "sterling area." With the development of the closer links with Spain and the repeal of the Exchange Control Act in the United Kingdom, it is generally thought that such fears can now be discounted.

Licences are required to carry on a banking or insurance business, and these are granted sparingly. But no licence is required to carry on a trust business, and an exempt company may act as a trustee of a settlement.

An exempt company in Gibraltar can be formed for £450 ($720). The annual tax or licence fee payable is at a flat rate of £225 in the case of an exempt company incorporated in

Gibraltar which is ordinarily resident in Gibraltar. Alternatively, an exempt company may pay income tax at the rate of 2 per cent. on income not remitted to Gibraltar and 27 per cent. on income remitted to Gibraltar; this option may be advantageous to clients whose own tax jurisdiction affords a more lenient treatment to shareholders in offshore companies which suffer local tax on their profits. Of more general interest is the facility, introduced in 1983, for companies registered outside Gibraltar to qualify for exempt status. Foreign companies pay a higher annual fee of £300 (U.S.$480), but the combination of incorporation in a less restrictive jurisdiction and management on the ground in Gibraltar can be a very valuable one, and this is an area where Gibraltar may expect to see a considerable growth of business.

One should not omit to mention that Gibraltar, like other British and formerly British jurisdictions referred to elsewhere in this book, does not tax locally incorporated companies which are resident elsewhere on income arising outside Gibraltar, but in the light of the freedom from tax conferred upon a resident company by an exemption, these considerations seem to be largely of theoretical interest.

Gibraltar is also an appropriate jurisdiction for the establishment of trusts. Their trust law is based on that of England, and includes provisions for the variation of trusts similar to those found in the English legislation. This is one of the aspects of the offshore services industry which the government is keen to encourage, and indeed the legislature enacted in 1986 a helpful (but not a very well drafted) ordinance which extended the perpetuity and accumulation periods to 100 years. The income of a Gibraltar trust of which the beneficiaries are non-resident and which arises outside Gibraltar is not charged to income tax in Gibraltar; this is not a matter of concession, but is enshrined in the law.

Mention should also be made of the so-called "hybrid company." As in England, a company may be incorporated in Gibraltar which is limited by guarantee, but there is nothing in the law of Gibraltar, as there is in the laws of the United Kingdom, which prevents a company limited by guarantee from having shareholders. İnternational tax planners have found interesting opportunities for companies which have both guarantors and shareholders, the guarantors (whose identity is not public knowledge) being entitled to the true equity of the company.

Hong Kong

The British Crown Colony of Hong Kong is a tax haven because its tax system (like that of Panama) has a territorial base. A company's residence or place of incorporation is generally immaterial: income with a source outside Hong Kong is not as a general rule subject to tax. Source is in the case of income from personal exertions determined by a "substantial operations" test which looks to the place of performance of the operations from which the profit in substance derive. Hong Kong is an important trading and manufacturing centre, well equipped with banking and professional services, and companies pay tax on their local income at the rate of only 18 per cent.. But its advantages have been overshadowed by two recent developments—the agreement for the return of Hong Kong to China in 1997 and the Hong Kong government's need to raise increased revenue from taxation.

Under the terms of the Joint Declaration by the governments of the United Kingdom and the People's Republic of China, China will "resume the exercise of sovereignty over Hong Kong with effect from 1st July 1997" and Hong Kong will become a Special Administrative Region of the People's Republic. The Joint Declaration states, however, that for 50 years Hong Kong will continue to retain its existing economic, social and legal systems, and that the "laws currently in force in Hong Kong will remain basically unchanged" (though with a final court of appeal in Hong Kong replacing appeals to the Privy Council in London); the government in Beijing "will not levy taxes on the Hong Kong Special Administrative Region," which "will retain the status of an international financial centre," and "there will be free flow of capital." Despite these assurances, it remains to be seen how far Hong Kong can maintain its present economic status and economic system after British administration ends; up till now no tax haven has flourished under communist rule.

China has very strong economic and diplomatic reasons for observing the terms of the Joint Declaration, not least of which are Hong Kong's contribution to China's economic development and the example offered to Taiwan if Hong Kong's prosperity and independence are retained, but the temptation to interfere in the administration of the Special Administrative Region may yet prove too strong.

While the return to China is still in the future, the effect of the other development has already been felt. The Hong Kong government has traditionally kept its expenditure low and met this expenditure chiefly by sales of land leases. In recent years, expenses of government have increased and revenue from land sales has fallen. The drop in revenue is due partly to a fall in land values and partly to a restriction in the Joint Declaration on the amount of land which may be sold each year. The Hong Kong goverment has therefore sought to increase revenue from taxation. This was seen in the rates of Profits Tax from 1984 to 1986, and in moves to broaden the tax base, partly by legislation and partly by seeking court decisions favourable to an extension of the concept of local source. However, 1986 was a very successful year for Hong Kong's economy, and resulted in a cut in the rate of all taxes on income. If the present prosperity continues, there will be scope for further reductions. The Hong Kong government has never actively sought tax haven status and successive Financial Secretaries have explained that any advantages of Hong Kong for international tax planning arise simply from the special circumstances of its tax system and the skills of its inhabitants. Nevertheless, the tax haven activities of the Colony are of significant economic importance, and it seems unlikely that the present administration will do them serious damage.

At the present time therefore the use of Hong Kong may be considered by clients of two kinds—first, those with short term activities which will have run their course by the early 1990s, and who either generate income with a source outside Hong Kong or regard 18 per cent. tax as acceptable, and secondly, those with longer term activities which involve no major commitment of fixed assets in the territory and would not suffer if Chinese tax officials were to gain access to the records (bearing in mind that China is developing a network of double taxation agreements, all of which provide for exchange of information between revenue authorities).

Hong Kong enjoys excellent communications with the rest of the world, including several daily flights into and out of Kai Tak airport from Europe, America and Australia. (Landings at Kai Tak can be hair-raising especially for those with window seats). There is no exchange control, and the Hong Kong dollar is presently pegged to the United States dollar (though this may change in the near future). The legal system derives from English law with some local modifications; English is widely spoken and all major international law firms, accountancy firms and most leading banks have representation in Hong Kong. Legal entities which are recognised include companies (the legislation is based on that of the United Kingdom prior to 1948), partnerships and trusts (though, curiously, these are little used in Hong Kong tax planning).

Since it is one of the world's major trading and manufacturing centres and a service centre for the region, the location of an office or subsidiary in Hong Kong can often be justified to foreign revenue authorities on commercial grounds, particularly where an enterprise is operating into China. Hong Kong government permission is not required for non-residents to set up a branch or subsidiary in Hong Kong, though a branch must register with the Registrar of Companies. A company established in Hong Kong may have all of its shareholders and directors non-resident and meetings may all be held outside the Colony (but it must have a resident secretary); bearer shares can be issued by public companies but not by private companies. Accounts must be audited. Annual returns must be filed for Hong Kong companies giving the names of directors and shareholders, but nominees can be used. Public companies must file accounts. Directors need not be resident in Hong Kong, but the company must have a resident secretary. A minimum of two shareholders is required. A General Meeting of the shareholders must be held every calendar year. A Hong Kong company can be incorporated for about U.S.$1,000; "off-the-shelf" companies are available. All branches, subsidiaries, partnerships and representative offices in Hong Kong must register as a business and a business registration fee (currently H.K.$650) (U.S.$80) is payable. Licences are required for banks and are granted sparingly to branches or subsidiaries of foreign banks. Many foreign banks operate as licensed or registered deposit-taking companies (which have restrictions on taking deposits from the public). Moreover, Hong Kong is an attractive location for expatriate staff or to hold meetings. While cultural activities are still relatively few (the annual spring arts festival is usually a sell-out well in advance), Hong Kong remains a paradise for shoppers and for devotees of Chinese cuisine. Taiwan, Japan, Macao, Mainland China, the Philippines and South-East Asia are all easily accessible and offer distractions for expatriates who feel they must escape from the Colony.

Hong Kong does not tax dividends, capital gains or interest paid by financial institutions. There are no customs duties except specific excise taxes on a narrow range of goods. Stamp duty is payable on, *inter alia*, assignments of Hong Kong shares, and there is a 0.6 per cent. capital duty on the share capital of a limited company incorporated in Hong Kong. Estate Duty is payable, but only on assets located in the Colony.

Although Hong Kong imposes income tax it has no double taxation agreements. No agreements means that there are no provisions for the exchange of information, and the Hong Kong Inland Revenue can suffer strict penalties for infringing taxpayers' confidentiality. On the other hand, there are no treaty provisions protecting income or capital from taxation or providing for credit for tax. Hong Kong's domestic legislation has only very limited provisions for foreign tax credits, which apply only to certain Commonwealth countries' taxes and to taxes on interest earned by financial institutions. Hong Kong relies primarily on its territorial tax base to avoid conflicts with other taxing jurisdictions. This has created problems recently where China has sought to tax the salaries of employees working in the Mainland, and some degree of local relief against double taxation is likely to be introduced in the near future.

The Isle of Man

The Isle of Man is an island of over 200 square miles, lying in the North Sea between Ireland to the west and England and Scotland to the east. Douglas, its principal town, has the period charm of slightly upmarket Blackpool. Though its history and character are very different, it has, from a constitutional and fiscal point of view, much in common with the Channel Islands. Like them, it is not part of the United Kingdom. The Queen of England is the monarch by virtue of her title of Lord of Man; local government is in the hands of an elected body, Tynwald. Income tax is levied at a standard rate of 20 per cent., but non-resident companies are, as in the United Kingdom, outside the charge to tax on their non-Manx income, and a concessionary exemption from tax on non-Manx income is afforded to trusts whose beneficiaries reside outside the Isle of Man. As in the Channel Islands, it is the trust and the non-resident company which has formed the backbone of the island's offshore business but captive insurance and ship registration are becoming of increasing significance.

The main entity used for offshore business activities has traditionally been the non-resident company limited by shares. This pays a fixed annual duty of £450 (U.S.$720); its income arising outside the island is tax-free. The Isle of Man also has its "exempt company." This is similar to its namesake in Gibraltar, except that its business must be restricted to the purchase and sale of commodities, the making of investments, the sale and purchase of investments, or the owning or chartering of ships. An exempt company pays an annual licence fee of £250 ($400). Its secretary and at least one director must be resident in the Isle of Man; no such rule applies to other companies.

For any company, two subscribers are required. Shares must have a par value. Ordinary shares cannot be bought into treasury without the consent of the court, but mutual funds or "open-ended" investment companies are allowed to redeem participating preference shares. Shares may be registered or bearer. The company's name must end with the word "Limited." At least two directors are required; corporate directors are not permitted. The names of the directors, their nationalities, addresses and business occupations appear on the Companies' Register, and all business letters and trade circulars must carry the names of the directors (and their nationality if other than British), but there is no requirement for a company to have a local director. The company must be audited annually, but no statement of its financial situation is included in its annual return. Under previous legislation, the *ultra vires* rule applied to the company's powers, and the Memorandum therefore set out its objects extensively. However, with effect from June 1, 1987, pursuant to the implementation of the Companies Act 1986, the need for objects in the Memorandum of Association of a company has been abolished. The presumption now will be that a company can do anything unless it is specifically restricted in the Memorandum of Association. "Off-the-shelf" companies are available. Special provisions apply to banking and insurance business (see below), but otherwise the company may carry on any kind of lawful business, including trust business. The cost of incorporating an Isle of Man company is about £400 ($640).

Manx company law is modelled on that of the United Kingdom, and makes provision for the incorporation of unlimited companies and companies limited by guarantee. In conformity with EEC practice, capital duty of 1 per cent. is levied on the issue of shares in a limited company up to a maximum duty of £50,000. This does not apply to unlimited companies. Unlimited companies have, of course, the disadvantage that the liability of members for the debts of the company is unlimited, but this may be of no consequence where the shareholders are limited companies (in whatever jurisdiction they are established) and the unlimited company has the advantage that its ordinary shares are freely redeemable. The company limited by guarantee can also be a most useful vehicle. The identity of the guarantors is not made public, and in jurisdictions (such as the United Kingdom) where a distinction is drawn for some tax purposes between shares and other forms of participation in the company, the rights of a guarantor may not be regarded as a "share," even though they confer on a guarantor an equity participation in the company's income and gains. As in Gibraltar, a company in the Isle of Man may be limited both by shares and by guarantee.

A government licence is required to carry on a banking or investment management business in the Isle of Man. A full banking licence is in practice only granted to banks of international standing and their subsidiaries. A more welcoming approach is adopted to investment management businesses, and to captive and other companies conducting an offshore insurance business. Rules made under the Exempt Insurance Companies Act provide for minimum share capital, solvency margins, the submission of accounts, the approval of directors, management and reinsurance arrangements and an annual licence fee. The whole of a company's underwriting risk must be located outside the Isle of Man. An insurance company complying with these rules is exempt from Manx tax on all its profits, and pays an annual fee of £2,000 ($3,200).

The trust law of the Isle of Man follows the English pattern. A trustee resident in the Isle of Man is in principle subject to Manx tax on the income of the trust property, but, as in the Channel Islands and other taxing jurisdictions which wish to attract offshore trust business, a concessionary exemption is granted to trusts where the settlor and beneficiaries reside outside the Isle of Man and the trust income is from sources outside the Isle of Man.

The Isle of Man has a tax treaty with the United Kingdom. It is an old treaty of limited scope, like those between Guernsey and Jersey and the United Kingdom, and does not, of course, apply to non-resident companies. It does, however, have provisions for exchange of information between the taxing authorities of the two jurisdictions. Like the Channel Islands, the Isle of Man is associated with the

EEC and enjoys the right of free trade in agricultural and industrial products. Unlike the Channel Islands, it is in complete customs union with the United Kingdom and has a value added tax identical to its U.K. counterpart.

Liberia

Liberian companies, like those incorporated in Panama, have been for many years convenient zero-tax vehicles. They have been much used in shipping, but are able to conduct international business of all kinds. Users of a Liberian company do not need to know much about Liberia; many of them could not draw the country's position on a map. The only contact required is the maintenance of a registered agent. Enterprises which specialise in the provision of Liberian companies have offices in New York, London and elsewhere. "Off-the-shelf" companies are available.

Liberia's system of law is modelled on that of the United States and the interpretations of U.S. Courts are commonly relied upon. The official language is English and the U.S. dollar is legal tender. There are no exchange controls. A Liberian corporation is not liable to local tax, so long as 75 per cent. of the shares are held by non-residents who are not Liberian nationals and the company's income is derived from sources outside Liberia.

The present law governing corporations was enacted in 1976 and provides a wide measure of freedom from restrictions and reporting requirements. Directors and other officers may be of any nationality and residence. Meetings of shareholders and directors may be held anywhere, or resolutions may be passed by unanimous written consent, without a meeting. The company may keep its records in any country. There are trust companies and registered agents which attend to all the necessary formalities.

Shares may be in registered or bearer form. If the articles of incorporation authorise the issue of bearer shares, they must provide for the manner in which any required notice shall be given to the shareholders. Changes in directors, officers and shareholders are not required to be entered on the public register. The registered agent is not obliged to file with Government any reports regarding corporate activities.

The constitution of a company is in English. A company may be incorporated by a single shareholder. The constitution of the company may express its objects in general terms—*i.e.* to engage in any lawful activity or act. The authorised share capital must be stated, but this may be amended from time to time. The capital may be in any currency. Shares may be issued with or without a par value.

The company must have a registered agent in Liberia, but does not require any other kind of presence there. In general, the minimum number of directors is three but if there are only two beneficial owners, then only two directors are required, and if there is only one beneficial owner, only one director is necessary. Directors need not be named in the articles, and there is no obligation to register subsequent changes in directors.

An extremely useful feature of Liberian corporate legislation is that it permits the company's name to include any words or abbreviations indicating that it is a limited company—*e.g.* Corporation, Company, Limited, Limitada, Societe Anonyme, Societe par actions, Sociedad Anonima, Aktiengesellschaft, Corp., Inc., Ltd., Ltda., S.A., A.G., A/S, N.V., Plc., A.B. The name of the company may be in any language. A company may change its name by filing Articles of Amendment. There is no minimum capital requirement. The company must keep adequate records and accounts but these do not need to be filed or audited. The Ministry of Foreign Affairs in Liberia will, upon request, issue a certificate of good standing, bearing its seal, providing evidence from the public records of Liberia of the existence of a corporation.

The government fees and charges are low: upon incorporation, a fee of $100 is payable to Government and $150 to the statutory Registered Agent, and similar fees are payable annually. A small additional fee will be payable on incorporation if the company's capital exceeds 500 shares of no par value or shares with a par value of more than $50,000, but if it does not, the total cost of incorporation, including the first year's fees, should not be more than $700.

Liechtenstein

Liechtenstein is a mountainous country, lying on the right bank of the Rhine between Switzerland and Austria. It is some 16 miles long and averages less than four miles wide. Communication by air is via Zurich, and main line trains to Vienna stop at Buchs, from which it is a short journey by road to Vaduz, the capital city. It has a customs union with Switzerland and its currency is the Swiss Franc. The language of the country is German, though English is often used in commercial transactions and widely spoken and understood in the business and the professional community. Like Switzerland, Liechtenstein enforces bank secrecy, the Bank Law providing heavy sanctions for any breach of professional secrecy. Liechtenstein has benefited for many years from its central situation in Europe, its sound economic position, the hard Swiss currency and the stable political situation. It has a Prince in a castle, delightful mountain scenery and an atmosphere of touristified Ruritania, remote from the stresses and complexities of the late twentieth century. The government has not permitted international banks, trust companies and other institutions to have a foothold in the Principality, and in practice much of Liechtenstein's offshore business is conducted out of offices in Zurich.

The available entities are numerous. The law concerning them—the *Personen-und Gesellschaftsrecht* (the "P.G.R.")—was enacted in 1926, long before statutory drafting became a branch of marketing. To get any kind of a grip on the P.G.R. is an intellectual task not lightly to be undertaken, especially for those whose mother tongue is not German, but this has not prevented certain Liechtenstein entities from acquiring a wide popularity. These are the Establishment (*Anstalt*), the Trust Enterprise or Business Trust (*Treuunternehmen*) and the Foundation (*Stiftung*).

The Anstalt functions as a kind of one-man company or incorporated pocket book. It is a legal entity with limited liability. It does not in general have any persons corresponding to shareholders; the founder is a kind of sole shareholder, and the holder of the founder's rights—which are assignable—is the supreme authority of the Anstalt, with unlimited power, in effect, to determine what the Anstalt does and who benefits from it. The founder may be of any nationality, and he may be a nominee for, or subsequently assign the founder's rights to, the person intending to enjoy these rights. Its name must contain the word "Anstalt," or its English, French or Italian equivalent, and the law does not permit a name which is untrue, immoral or illegal or which contributes to unfair competition. The articles of incorporation contain, as well as the name of the Anstalt, its objects and purposes, its capital, its organisation and structure, the principles governing its accounts and balance sheet and the method by which its notices are to be published. The articles also contain provisions for the liquidation and dissolution of the Anstalt. The articles may be changed subsequently.

The minimum capital is 30,000 Swiss Francs (U.S.$19,700), or its equivalent in foreign currency. The articles must provide for a Board of Directors, of which one member must be resident in Liechtenstein and licensed by the government. If the Anstalt is to engage in commercial activities, it must have a duly qualified and licensed auditor, and audited accounts must be submitted to the tax administration. All non-commercial Anstalts must draw up an annual statement of assets and liabilities and the Liechtenstein member of the board must confirm its availability to the public register every year.

The founder may provide in the by-laws of the Anstalt for other persons to benefit from its assets or income, in addition to or to the exclusion of himself. If he does so, the Anstalt takes on a character which, in Anglo-Saxon terms, is closer to a trust than a company.

On formation, an Anstalt is liable to formation duty of 3 per cent. of its capital, together with a registration fee of 500 francs (U.S.$330) for a capital up to 100,000 francs (U.S.$65,800) and 150 francs for each additional 100,000 francs. Anstalts which carry on activities within the country are liable to pay taxes on their capital and on their profits. But if an Anstalt does not engage in any economic activities within Liechtenstein, it is not liable to pay tax on its profits, and is only liable to pay 0.1 per cent. tax on capital and reserves subject to a minimum liability of 1,000 francs (U.S.$660) per annum. This tax is payable each year in advance.

The authorities are entitled to inspect book-keeping records of all corporate bodies. An Anstalt with a non-commercial purpose, (e.g. holding investments) is not required to submit any accounts to the tax authorities, but merely to have a statement of assets and liabilities available for inspection by the Registrar. The Registrar does not appear in practice to exercise this right, and Anstalts commonly pay the minimum annual tax of S.frs.1,000.

The business trust is modelled on the American Business Trust. In the form in which it is commonly used, it is a kind of incorporated settlement, a separate legal entity with limited liability. Although the business trust is, as a matter of law, quite distinct from the Anstalt, it operates in a similar way and is taxed similarly.

Foundations and Trusts have become more widely used than Anstalts. The Foundation is a legal entity with an unlimited period of existence. Like an English trust, it has beneficiaries. There is a board of directors which appoints the beneficiaries and determines the distributions to them. In certain circumstances it is not necessary to have the Foundation registered in the Liechtenstein public register. The minimum capital of a Foundation is S.frs.30,000; it is taxed like an Anstalt, but with reduced rates on assets over S.frs.2,000,000.

Trusts in Liechtenstein are of two kinds. A trust may be interpreted entirely in accordance with the law of Liechtenstein, where the P.G.R. has attempted to codify, with some variants, the English rules of equity. Or the trust may, while being governed by the law of Liechtenstein, be required to be interpreted in accordance with some foreign law—e.g. of

England or that of New York. Practitioners from common law jurisdictions will be inclined to feel on firmer ground with this second kind of trust. A trust of either kind is taxed in the same way as the Anstalt.

Luxembourg

The Grand Duchy of Luxembourg is a country some 50 miles long and 35 miles wide, with frontiers with Belgium, France and Germany. Formerly heavily dependent on its steel industry, it has in recent years become an important centre for banks and investment companies. It is a tax haven only in one respect, and that is that it has—and has had since the late 1920s—legislation which permits the establishment of a holding company not subject to income tax.

A holding company may engage only in a limited number of activities. It may acquire, hold and sell or otherwise exploit shares, stocks and patents. It may control and administer its investments from Luxembourg, but it may not run a commercial business open to the public, nor may it own land or property except for the purpose of providing itself with offices, nor act as a commission agent or broker.

A holding company is generally a company limited by shares. At least two shareholders are required; shares may be in registered or bearer form. A minimum of three directors is required, but there is no restriction on their nationality. The company must appoint an auditor and deposit every year an abbreviated financial statement with the district court. The share capital may be expressed in Luxembourg Francs (which are on a par with the Belgian Franc) or in any other currency.

A Luxembourg holding company is a relatively expensive vehicle. There is a capital duty of 1 per cent., payable to the government, and there are various initial costs, including the costs of registration, publication and notarisation, apart from the fees of the professional advisers involved. There are significant annual costs also, filing quarterly returns, holding annual meetings in Luxembourg, maintaining accounts and share registers at the registered office in Luxembourg and publication of financial statements in the official journal. In addition there is an annual tax on the issued capital. It is at the modest rate of 0.2 per cent., but it is levied on the aggregate market value of the company's issued shares. In the case of unquoted companies, the market value of the shares is taken to be whichever is the larger of the nominal capital or an amount equal to 10 times the total dividend paid in respect of the previous year, so that there is an effective tax rate of at least 2 per cent. on dividends.

Luxembourg is essentially a jurisdiction for the company which has or foresees some form of public participation in its share capital—companies holding portfolios of quoted and unquoted securities, and companies with wholly-owned subsidiaries carrying on businesses in other parts of the world and functioning together as a group. The use of the holding company form may be allied with a quotation on the Luxembourg Stock Exchange. Luxembourg is not a market place of the nature of Vancouver, New York or London, but it is a respected financial centre, and the listing of a holding company there can confer a certain standing on the group as a whole.

Luxembourg holding companies do not benefit from the tax treaties to which Luxembourg is a party. For this it is necessary to have a taxpaying company. Under the treaties between Luxembourg and Belgium, Ireland, the United Kingdom and the United States, a taxpaying company can receive interest free of withholding tax in those countries. Luxembourg does not impose income tax on outgoing interest, so that the classic "stepping stone" transaction involves a loan from a zero-tax vehicle to a Luxembourg company, which lends onwards to the ultimate borrower in Belgium, Ireland, the United Kingdom or the United States. The practice is to leave a normal commercial profit, which, as a guide (and depending on the amount involved), might be between one-sixteenth and one-eighth per cent., in the taxpaying company. The end result of the transaction is that the zero-tax vehicle receives interest indirectly out of these high tax jurisdictions, without deduction of the withholding tax which it would suffer if it received the interest directly. A Luxembourg holding company may be used as the zero-tax vehicle: in such a structure, one has two Luxembourg companies—one paying tax on the one–sixteenth to one-eighth per cent, less expenses, and the other a holding company, receiving, and, if required, accumulating interest free of tax.

A law of August 25, 1983, introduced a legal framework for mutual funds. These are taxed more favourably than holding companies: instead of the 1 per cent. tax on capital contribution, they pay a flat duty of L.Frcs.50,000 (U.S.$1,350) and they are subject to an annual duty of 0.06 per cent. (though on the net worth of their portfolios rather than on the market value of their shares).

Monaco

"A sunny place for shady people." The phrase is too amusing to be forgotten, but, however true it was in Somerset Maugham's day, there is now no reason to suppose that the little Principality on the south coast of France contains more than a statistically average proportion of scoundrels. Indeed, quite the contrary. Gone are the Frenchmen evading tax with brassplate Monegasque companies along the Boulevard des Moulins. A resident's visa is issued to foreigners only after due enquiry, and woe betide the successful applicant who only pretends to live in the Principality, for fiscal or other reasons, and actually lives elsewhere.

What fiscally distinguishes the Principality from the rest of Europe (leaving aside Sark and Albania) is the absence of income tax on the income of individuals. Monegasque companies trading outside the Principality pay corporation tax at 35 per cent. and Monaco has the French system of value added tax, but its freedom from personal income tax has attracted a number of "tax exiles," and makes it possible for local enterprises to remunerate some extremely expensive talent more handsomely (or, to look at it another way, more economically) than is possible elsewhere in Europe.

Monaco has its own trust law. This does not attempt to codify the English rules of equity, but simply permits foreigners to establish in Monaco trusts which are to be interpreted in accordance with the law of their country of citizenship. This is a little-known facility, which perhaps deserves to be more widely recognised. But trusts are not the growing-point of Monaco's present offshore activities: this lies in the management in Monaco of companies which are incorporated elsewhere. As the reader of this book will already know, there are many jurisdictions—those which derive their system of taxation from the United Kingdom—which do not tax companies incorporated under their laws on their foreign income, so long as the companies are not "managed and controlled" there. "Management and control" is not a criterion for taxability in Monaco, and Monaco has therefore proved an attractive location for this kind of "management and control." It has proved an attractive base also for the management and control of companies whose jurisdiction of incorporation is indifferent to management and control but which is too remote from the European centres in which their effective managers are situated. Thus, companies incorporated in Hong Kong, Liberia and Panama are managed in Monaco for practical rather than fiscal reasons. The Principality has the advantage that if one is going to have a meeting, this is one of the more agreeable places to have it, and the director who might find reasons to put off a meeting in the Cayman Islands or the Isle of Man will find time in his diary for a couple of nights at the Hermitage or down the road at the Voile d'Or.

There are nowadays companies in Monte Carlo which provide an administration and management service for foreign companies. A degree of circumspection is evidently requisite. The name of a foreign company is not blazoned on the door or otherwise made visible outside the office; its name does not appear in the telephone directory; and postal communication to it is directed care of the management company concerned. But so long as the commercial activities of the foreign company take place wholly outside Monaco, there is no occasion for local tax to be chargeable on its profits. The profit of the local management company, arising from the fees it charges for its services, is of course subject to Monegasque tax at the 35 per cent. rate. Costs tend to be on the high side: the charge for providing two local directors and basic administration in Monaco will be not less than $1,500.

For all its independent status, the government of Monaco is not going to do anything which seriously displeases Paris, and some of the circumspection may have been due in the past to a sense that, in French eyes, while the management of foreign companies in Monaco was lawful, it was not exactly an activity which Government ought to encourage. It

has been felt recently, however, that more encouraging sig-
nals are coming from Paris, and that in the present climate of
deregulation and market forces, the French government is
conscious that it could be an advantage to them to have an
offshore centre, which is culturally though not politically
part of France, and that the French economy, and in particular the financial services sector in Paris, may benefit from the
flow of inward investment capable of being attracted
through Monaco. What developments in this area will take
place remains to be seen, but at all events the attitude of the
Monegasque government itself to the offshore services
industry seems to have changed from tolerance to encour-
agement.

Nauru

Nauru is a Pacific island, tiny and rich in phosphate deposits. It lies on the Equator and is miles from anywhere. But it is an independent Republic and a member of the British Commonwealth, and since 1972 it has offered facilities for the incorporation of zero-tax companies.

English is taught in schools and the law follows English patterns. The currency is the Australian dollar, but there is no exchange control. There are no accountants or lawyers available on the island, but incorporation and administration of companies is handled by two corporation agents and the Nauru Government Commercial Authority. The government of Nauru imposes no internal taxes of any kind, and, since the phosphate deposits are far from exhausted, sees no prospect of needing to do so.

Two kinds of companies are available. There are those which are designed simply to hold the investments of a single person or of a small group of persons, in relation to which minimal disclosure is required. These are called "holding corporations." And those which can enter into commercial transactions, and may, subject to statutory safeguards, offer their shares to the public. These are called "trading corporations."

A holding corporation may be incorporated with a single shareholder. Its shares may be in registered or bearer form; the maximum number of shareholders is 20, and if the shares are in bearer form not more than 20 of them may be in issue at any time. The shares must have a par value. A holding corporation may purchase its own shares, so long as it remains solvent, and so long as the purchase money comes out of earned or capital surplus. There are no restrictions on the corporate name. The company must have a registered secretary: this is a corporation registered in Nauru for the purpose, of which there are presently four. It is usual for the company to have a registered director, but this is not necessary, and no minimum number of directors is prescribed. The company must keep accounts, but there are no provisions requiring audit currently in force.

A holding corporation must not carry on any trade nor invite any investment from the public. A corporation must file an annual return with the Registrar, but the information contained in it may be disclosed only to members, debenture holders, directors or a liquidator of the company and not to the public.

A trading corporation is subject to fewer restrictions, but more information about it is made public. At least two shareholders are required. These may be either individuals or companies. As with holding corporations, the shares must have a par value, but may be in registered or bearer form. Trading corporations are not free to purchase their own shares. A trading corporation must have at least two directors: one of them will generally be a registered director but at least one of them must not be. A company may be a director. A registered secretary is required. A trading corporation must keep accounts and render annual returns, which are filed with the Registrar and open to public inspection. A licence is required to carry on a banking business. A licence for a "captive" bank may be obtained. A licence is also required for an insurance company and will be granted to suitable applicants. A licence is required for a trust corporation; a "captive" trust corporation may be possible, but it is understood that an unrestricted licence is unlikely to be granted.

The name of a trading corporation or holding corporation requires the approval of the Registrar. It must end in Corporation, Corp., Incorporated, or Inc. In the name of a holding corporation the penultimate word must be Holding or Holdings; neither of these words may form part of a name of a trading corporation.

The Netherlands Antilles

The Netherlands Antilles comprise several islands in the Caribbean, widely separated from each other. They are part of the Kingdom of the Netherlands, with internal self-government. They have a civil law system, similar to that of the Netherlands in Europe. The language is Dutch, though English is much used (and generally spoken in St. Maarten). The currency is the Netherlands Antilles Guilder (N.A.fl.). The current rate of exchange is N.A.fl.1 = US$0.56. There is exchange control, but companies formed by non-residents and not engaged in local business are exempt from it. Most of the international business is done in Curacao, which lies off the coast of South America. It is also possible (and more agreeable) to do international business in St. Maarten, which is much further north.

The feature of the Netherlands Antilles which interests the international tax planner is the combination of low tax rates and the benefits of tax treaties. The general rate of tax on corporations is 27 per cent.–34 per cent., together with a municipal surtax. Certain kinds of companies, however, are exempt from the municipal surtax and pay tax at the rates of 2.4 per cent. on the first N.A.fl.100,000 (which is about U.S.$56,000) and 3 per cent. on the residue of their net taxable income. Such companies are also free of tax on their capital gains. The law guarantees the continuance of this regime until 1999.

This regime applies to investment companies holding shares, bonds and other securities. It also applies to companies receiving royalties and rentals in respect of patents, copyrights, trademarks, designs, land and real property and the use of industrial, commercial and scientific equipment. The net fees from rendering technical assistance outside the Antilles are similarly taxed. The Netherlands Antilles imposes no withholding or other taxes on dividends and interest paid to non-residents, and shares held by non-residents are not subject to any estate or inheritance tax.

Tax treaties exist between the Netherlands Antilles and the Netherlands, Norway, the United Kingdom and the United States. Of much the greatest importance is the treaty with the United States: it has been extensively used by U.S. corporations to raise money on the Eurobond market via an Antilles subsidiary, and by non-resident aliens for inward investments into the United States. This is a subject about which there is a great deal to be known, most of it nowadays rather discouraging, and some or all of it obsolescent, for there are signs at the time of writing that the new treaty, which has been under negotiation since 1980, will soon come into effect. The United Kingdom treaty excludes Antilles companies which enjoy the privileged tax regime from benefiting under the articles relating to dividends, interest and royalties. Such companies, however, continue to enjoy the benefit of the article exempting commercial profits in the absence of a permanent establishment, and Antilles companies have been much used by non-residents for property transactions in the United Kingdom. Under the treaty with the Netherlands, dividends from a Netherlands company can, by the interposition of a Netherlands Antilles parent company, reach the ultimate shareholders subject to a tax charge which is significantly lower than that achievable by any other route, and this is extremely advantageous where the Netherlands company, because of the participation privilege, or because the source of its income is in a low-tax jurisdiction outside the Netherlands, suffers little or no tax on its corporate profits, but nevertheless enjoys the benefit of treaties to which the Netherlands is a party. The tax charge on dividends from companies in Norway may likewise be reduced by the interposition of a Netherlands parent.

As in the Netherlands itself, it is possible in the Antilles to discuss a prospective transaction with the tax authorities and to obtain a ruling which will determine its tax treatment. Where offshore business is concerned, the tax authorities in the Antilles are inclined to take a generous view of the deduction of such items as interest and depreciation, so that a company which opts to pay the full rate of tax, so as not to be debarred from enjoying the benefits of the U.K. or U.S. treaty, may pay a high rate of tax on a low income.

A minimum of two subscribers is needed to form a company in the Netherlands Antilles. The Articles of Incorporation are in Dutch. They require to be approved by the Ministry of Justice. Approval may nowadays be obtained in two or three days. "Off the shelf" companies are available—at a price. Shares may be in bearer or registered form, but must have a par value. Shares may be redeemed, provided that at least 20 per cent. of the authorised capital remains outstanding. The name of the company must end in "Naamloze Vennootschap," or its abbreviation, "N.V."

There is no minimum of directors, and corporate directors are permitted, but the company must have a General Manager—the equivalent of a managing director—who is resident in the Netherlands Antilles. An audit is not required, but accounts must be kept and a financial statement prepared annually which accompanies the company's tax return. Financial information about the company is not generally available to the public, but in certain cases— notably where bearer shares are issued for over N.A.fl.50,000 (U.S.$28,000), or the company's securities are quoted on a stock exchange, or it is part of the company's business to borrow from third parties, or the company carries on an insurance business—these statements must be filed in the Commercial Register and are open to public inspection for eight days. A licence is readily obtainable for a company to carry on an offshore or captive insurance business, and a special tax regime applies to the profits of such businesses, the tax base for companies carrying on general insurance business being 10 per cent. of the offshore premiums. Annual meetings of the shareholders must be held in the Netherlands Antilles, but this may be done by proxy.

The incorporation cost of a Netherlands Antilles company includes a variety of charges—stamp taxes, publication costs, registration fee and notarial charges. A company with a capital of U.S.$30,000 will cost approximately $1,600. Annual maintenance costs typically amount to some $1,200 a year.

Panama

Panama is a kind of beginner's tax haven. It produces companies in enormous numbers—something like 120 every working day. They are easy, cheap and quick. They are available "off-the-shelf."

The Republic of Panama is a tropical country in Central America. With its important Canal, it enjoys and suffers a strong U.S. influence; its currency is the balboa, on a par with the U.S. dollar, but the country has no paper currency of its own, and the U.S. dollar bill is the medium of exchange. The official language is Spanish, but English is widely used and most company documents may be written in any language. It has a Free Zone, at the Atlantic entrance to the Canal. It is an important banking centre. But the country is best known for its companies.

Panama's income tax has a territorial base: income tax is not, and never has been, levied on income arising outside the country. Interest on money loaned for use abroad is treated as arising abroad. Profits from the purchase and sale of goods are treated as arising outside the country, so long as the goods are not at any time brought into the country. Directing operations which are completed, consummated or take effect abroad is treated as a source outside Panama. Dividends from companies whose income arises outside Panama are themselves treated as having a source outside Panama. Although it is possible, within these rules, for a company to conduct all kinds of banking and other international business from an office and with employees in Panama, the typical Panamanian company does nothing in Panama except pay its fees and costs. Shares in companies whose assets are largely situated outside Panama are not subject to inheritance tax.

Panamanian company law was adapted from the law of Delaware in 1927. It is the practice to have two incorporators; the identity of subsequent shareholders is not public knowledge. The shares may be in registered or bearer form and with or without a par value. Shares can be bought into treasury, so long as the price does not represent more than the value of the company's assets. The company's name must end with Sociedad Anonima, S.A., Corp., or Inc., but not with Limited or Ltd.

The company must have at least three directors, who need not be shareholders. Changes of directors are recorded. Directors may be of any nationality or residence, but the company is required to have a Resident Agent, who must be a practising attorney or a law firm. The company must also have a president, secretary and treasurer. These are appointed by the directors. They need not be shareholders or directors. One person may hold all three offices. A company not operating in Panama is not required to keep or file accounts. It must keep a minute book and share register, but these do not need to be kept in Panama. Special regulations apply to companies carrying on banking business or trust administration. The total cost of forming a Panamanian company (apart from the annual tax) is of the order of $800 to $1,000. There is an annual tax of $150 a year, and this, together with the services of the Registered Agent and three directors will, in a simple case, come to about $900 a year.

Switzerland

Switzerland has for many years offered holding companies, domiciliary companies and service companies, to which lower rates of tax are applied. They suffer a tax burden much heavier than do comparable entities described in other chapters of this book but, for many clients, their fiscal disadvantage is outweighed by the advantages of conducting business out of Switzerland. More competitive are the facilities offered by Switzerland for the administration of trusts and companies established under the laws of other jurisdictions.

The Swiss are well-accustomed to doing business with foreigners. Foreigners came on the Grand Tour and in the Simplon Orient Express; they came for their tuberculosis, to take waters and climb Alps; they came to deposit their valuables and cash in the vaults and numbered accounts of banks. A discreet, organised and assiduous financial services industry grew up to meet the needs of these clients. Being a client in Switzerland is rather like being a paying guest in a castle: so long as you obey the rules and pay the bill, your presence will be amicably tolerated, but you are not to bring the establishment into disrepute, and you are not to forget that an unbridgeable social gulf separates you from the proprietor.

Switzerland is a Confederation of 26 Cantons. It is not a member of the EEC, but Swiss industrial products enjoy free entry into the Community. Its law is civil: federal laws, which are relevant to most business matters, apply throughout the country, while criminal, civil and administrative procedure is governed by Cantonal laws. The official languages are French, German, Romansch and Italian, but English is generally well understood by people in business and the professions. The currency is the Swiss franc. There are no exchange controls.

Swiss companies are taxed at three levels—Federal, Cantonal and Communal. There are taxes on profits and net worth. The rate of the tax on profits depends upon the ratio between the company's profits and its capital, including reserves. The tax rate is high when the return on capital is high and lower when it is lower. Thus, Federal tax on company profits is levied at a rate between 3.63 per cent. and 9.8 per cent., the highest rate being reached when the return on capital exceeds 23 per cent. Cantonal rates are similarly calculated, and can be as much as 35 per cent. Communal taxes are calculated on the same principles.

The tax on the company's net worth (which excludes foreign real estate and the assets of a foreign permanent establishment) is levied at two levels—by the Federation at the rate of 0.0825 per cent. and by the Cantons, at rates which typically vary between 0.15 and 0.35 per cent.

A holding company is favourably treated at Federal level and in most Cantons. The company's investments in each case must amount to at least 20 per cent. of the capital of a domestic or foreign company or have a value of at least two million francs. If the whole of a company's income is derived from such investments, no tax is payable on it. The proceeds of liquidation of any of the companies whose shares are held by the holding company are treated in the same way, but capital gains on the disposal of such investments are not.

The majority of Cantons offer a statutory concession known as the "domiciliary" status and this applies to companies which maintain a registered office in Switzerland, but which have no commercial activity within the country and, generally, no permanent office staff, although certain Cantons (including Fribourg, Neuchatel and Valais) allow a company to maintain a small office staff and still qualify for the domiciliary privilege. Such a company would typically act as a European sales company for a group, or as a licensing or finance company, and in consequence of the domiciliary tax privilege it would, in a Canton such as Fribourg or Zug (which are two of the Cantons most favoured for this type of operation), be totally exempt from any Cantonal or municipal tax on its foreign income. Elsewhere, a small Cantonal capital tax, not exceeding a rate typically between 0.1

and 0.5 per cent. of the capital and reserves of the company, would be payable, and thus in effect such a company would be liable only to the Federal tax on net profits. For example, in the Canton of Vaud, companies which are foreign-controlled and whose commercial and industrial activities lie principally or exclusively outside Switzerland are regarded as domiciliary companies, and there special tax rules apply under which the company will pay Cantonal and communal taxes amounting together to 28 per cent. on only 20 per cent. of its net foreign profits, which gives an effective tax rate of 5.6 per cent.

Where a company's business activity necessitates an administrative office with personnel in significant numbers, or where the company engages in business in Switzerland and thus generates income from Swiss sources, the domiciliary privilege will not apply. In such a case the appropriate tax status is that known as a "mixed" company. This is a status which is granted in a number of Cantons, including (among others) Zug, Geneva, Vaud, Valais and Zurich. Under this tax status the company will generally be taxed at the ordinary Cantonal rate of 30 to 38 per cent. on its Swiss-source income and will be granted a special concessionary rate for its foreign-source income. For example, a company domiciled in Geneva will pay Cantonal tax on its Swiss-source income at ordinary rates of up to 35.7 per cent. but on its foreign-source income at only 9 per cent. In the Canton of Vaud, Swiss-source income will be taxable at rates of up to 28 per cent, while the foreign-source income may be taxed only to the extent of 20 per cent. of that income at the same 28 per cent. rate—that is, at 5.6 per cent. Such a company—in either Canton—would typically be the kind of European sales company which requires substantial local personnel. Similar rulings are also available for Swiss branch offices of foreign companies.

There is also a special status for Swiss companies which render finance, marketing, public relations or other services to related companies situated outside Switzerland. Such a company may often be a simple domiciliary company, but if it requires more extensive administrative facilities and local personnel than would be permitted under the domiciliary tax status, certain Cantons will offer it a special tax arrangement. Companies benefiting from such arrangements are known as "service" or "auxiliary" companies. With a company of this kind it may be difficult to determine its true profits, since the price charged for the services rendered to the foreign affiliated companies will not be accepted as being arrived at on an arm's-length basis for Swiss tax purposes. Cantons differ as to whether they will accept the book profits or whether they wish to make adjustments. Some Cantons require a minimum profit of 10 to 20 per cent. of overhead expenses to be declared, and the Federal tax administration has issued a circular to all the Cantonal tax administrations, which effectively requires that a company carrying on such an activity for affiliated companies should report income similar to that which an independent company would have realised. The circular also contains guidelines to the effect that the taxable profit should not be less than 10 per cent. of the expenses of the Swiss company, or one-sixth of its total payroll, together with taxable royalty and investment income.

Many Cantons have special provisions relating to the taxation of such companies, and other Cantons which do not have any specific statutory concessions will generally listen to any representations which may be made on behalf of a company intending to qualify as a service company. One of the features of the Swiss tax scene is that the Cantonal tax authorities are very approachable: they are prepared to listen to what a company wishes to do, and may issue a special tax ruling to cover the particular case.

These tax regimes, for holding, domiciliary, auxiliary and service companies may seem quite attractive until one takes into account the Federal withholding tax. This is levied at the rate of 35 per cent. on dividends and distributions. This may be reduced to as little as 5 per cent. under a treaty, but the *quid pro quo* for treaty relief will generally be the payment of tax in the treaty partner country. This tax may be postponed virtually indefinitely, if the company does not wish to distribute its profits. But it is hard to avoid the ultimate incidence of withholding tax. The tax is not suffered on the repatriation of profits earned by the Swiss branch or permanent establishment of a foreign company, but such branch or permanent establishment will generally be liable to full Swiss tax on profits as they are earned. No withholding tax is levied on interest paid in respect of ordinary commercial loans, or on rents, royalties or technical assistance fees, but where such payments exceed an arm's length consideration, the excess may be regarded as a constructive dividend. And there is very limited scope for utilising a Swiss company to take advantage of the treaties to which Switzerland is a partner and at the same time reducing the tax base of the company by outward payments ("the stepping stone" transaction). Although Switzerland is party to a large number of tax treaties, the 1962 Decree limits the extent to which deductions may be made against passive (but not business) income which enjoys the benefit of the treaty. In addition, at least 25 per cent. of such treaty—privileged income must be distributed by the Swiss corporate recipient in the form of a dividend.

One has to bear in mind the continuing difficulties of obtaining permits for foreign personnel. But the Swiss authorities have an essentially pragmatic approach to the question and are still prepared to grant favourable consideration to new businesses which wish to establish themselves in Switzerland, particularly if that business can be easily integrated into what is essentially a service economy in Switzerland, and if at the same time.

The new business will both generate employment for Swiss clerical and managerial personnel and make a significant contribution to the local revenue. Switzerland does not offer any tax concessions to foreign employees. On the other hand, the total of the normal Federal, Cantonal and communal taxes are not high by general European standards: for example, a married man living in Zurich, having a total income of 100,000 Swiss francs (U.S.$65,800), will pay tax at an average of 27 per cent. Marginal rates do not generally exceed 40 per cent. On top of the personal income tax, there is a social security levy which also goes towards pension contributions, levied at a flat rate of 10 per cent. on all salaries, of which one-half is payable by the employee and the other half by the employer. Company funded pension schemes are also now compulsory although the level of contributions required by both the employer and the employee need not necessarily exceed 5 per cent. of the salaries paid.

The type of company most generally used is the company limited by shares (*Société Anonyme*). Shares may be in registered or bearer form; they must have a par value. The minimum number of subscribers is three. Redemption of shares requires special authorisation, which will only be given if it can be shown that there will be no loss to creditors. There is no minimum number of directors, but corporate directors are not permitted, and a majority of the directors must be Swiss citizens residing in Switzerland. An audit is compulsory. Government approval is required for an investment trust, bank or insurance company. The identity of the directors and the place of the company's registered office are registered and open to public inspection, but no financial statements are available to the public, neither are the identities of the founders and subsequent shareholders.

Like other civil law countries, Switzerland does not have the concept of "management and control," and the mere fact that a company holds its board meetings in Switzerland does not of itself expose the company to any Swiss tax, though some advisers believe that it is not desirable to hold all board meetings in the same Canton. This opens up the possibility for a company whose profit is to be derived from operations carried on outside Switzerland to have its control and administration there, but to be incorporated, not under Swiss law, but under the law—say—of some part of the United Kingdom.

Switzerland does not have a law of trusts, but there is nothing to prevent a company with administrative offices in Switzerland or even a company incorporated under the law of a Swiss Canton from being appointed the trustee of a trust established under the law of some other jurisdiction. Where the trust income arises outside Switzerland and the beneficiaries reside outside Switzerland, the Swiss do not seek to impose any tax on the trust income. For a settlor based in Europe at any rate this is a most attractive option: if he wishes to establish, for example, a trust under the law of the Cayman Islands, he may find a trust company whose business is carried on in the Cayman Islands too remote and inaccessible, the difference in time zone making it impossible for him to communicate with his trustee before lunch. By appointing a co-trustee or an affiliate of the Cayman trustee to conduct the administration of the trust in Switzerland, he affords the trust fund all the benefits of the services of the Swiss financial sector, and he can more readily communicate with his trustee—and if required pay a personal visit to the office of his trustee at a few hours notice, while retaining the benefit of the Cayman Islands law on trusts and the liberty, if the tax position in Switzerland should at any time appear less favourable, of moving the administration of the trust to some other jurisdiction.

On the formation of a Swiss company, stamp duty of 3 per cent. is levied on the capital, and a registration fee which varies with the size of the capital of the company. The total cost of incorporating a company with the minimum share capital of 50,000 Swiss francs (U.S.$32,900) may come to about 6,000 francs (U.S.$3,950), and may cost between 2,000 and 5,000 francs (U.S.$1,300–3,290) a year to maintain.

The Swiss have a deep-rooted belief in the virtue of privacy, and disclosure of confidential information is not only in some instances punishable by law, but is wholly contrary to their custom. Article 47 of the Federal Banking Law makes divulgence of banking secrets a criminal offence. It is also a breach of a banker's civil duty to his client. Their tradition of confidentiality has been abused by people involved in the narcotics trade, organised crime and frauds of various kinds. Tax evasion is not a crime in Switzerland, but tax fraud is, and the Swiss court has been willing to allow information to be exchanged under a tax treaty where tax fraud is shown. Switzerland has a treaty with the United States for mutual assistance in criminal matters and an agreement with the United States designed to curb insider trading. The drift of

Swiss official opinion may be gauged from their willingness to block the Swiss assets of the former President of the Phillipines. Switzerland is anxious to co-operate with other nations in fighting crime, and the Swiss are aware that their traditional approach may need some modification.

Turks and Caicos Islands

In 1981, Turks and Caicos overhauled its company and banking laws, and rapidly acquired a reputation for quick and cheap incorporation in the context of what are essentially English laws and institutions. It is a British colony consisting of eight islands at the south-east tip of the Bahamas archipelago. The local currency is the U.S. dollar and there is no exchange control. There is no income tax or direct tax of any kind. The Confidential Relationships Ordinance of 1979 imposes a general duty of secrecy on persons in possession of confidential information, as does the Companies Ordinance 1981 in relation to exempted companies.

The kind of company most commonly used in Turks and Caicos is the company limited by shares. The law provides for two kinds of company—the ordinary company (which may be limited by shares or by guarantee or may be unlimited) and the exempted company (which must be limited by shares). For both kinds of company the incorporation procedure is simple and bearer shares and shares of no par value are permitted. A company must keep accounts but these are not available to the public.

The law providing for the exempted company embodies several features from the laws of other jurisdictions, in accordance with advice which was given to Government by distinguished practitioners in the international tax planning field. A company may qualify as exempted if its business is mainly outside the Colony. It may obtain from Government a 20 year guarantee against possible future taxes. It may be incorporated with a single subscriber. It may have redeemable shares and may exclude the *ultra vires* doctrine. Its name can be in any language and need not end in "Limited"; it may contain other designations—*e.g.* Inc., A.G., B.V., S.A., but need not. One director may form a quorum and corporate directors are permitted. Directors may reside anywhere, but the company must appoint a local agent, to be responsible for filing an annual Declaration of Compliance and to accept on behalf of the company service of any proceedings. There is no requirement for audit. An exempted company may transfer its domicile into and out of the islands; it need not file an annual return, nor is it required to maintain a register of or make public the identity of its directors or shareholders. There is no requirement for an annual general meeting. There is no minimum capital requirement. The capital may be expressed in any currency and may be multi-currency. In addition to the guarantee against future tax, the company may obtain a 20 year guarantee against future increases in annual company fees (presently $300 a year).

On incorporation, a registration fee is payable to Government, related to the company's authorised capital. For an exempted company the minimum is $325, for an ordinary company $275. Thereafter the annual fee is $300 for an exempted company and $250 for an ordinary company. The cost of incorporating a company of a conventional kind is about $700, plus the government fees. The annual cost of maintaining a registered office and company secretary is about $300 and a local agent normally charges $300 per annum.

No licence is required for the formation of a trust company. Bills were introduced in 1981 and 1987 to regulate insurance companies, but at the time of writing they have not been passed into law. There is a system of "A" and "B" licences for banks conducting domestic and offshore business respectively and for a "financial institution," which may conduct banking business but may not use the word "bank" in its title or in any published literature or documents.

Trusts and settlements of the kind known to English law may be established in Turks and Caicos under the general law. Some interesting supplementary provisions are contained in an Ordinance passed in 1985. Rather than enact an entire codified law of its own, the legislature gave the settlor the option of providing that the English law should apply to a settlement. The Ordinance also provides for trust companies in Turks and Caicos to be "approved" and the use of an approved trustee can give the trust certain advantages—excluding the rule against perpetuities, overcoming any lack of capacity of a settlor in accordance with the law of his domicile, providing for a form of statutory discretionary trust and empowering the Attorney-General to enforce the provisions of the trust. Trusts taking advantage of these provisions suffer a certain lack of mobility: although a trustee not within the jurisdiction of the court of the Turks and Caicos Islands may be appointed, the Attorney-General has power in effect to bring the trust back within that jurisdiction by himself appointing an approved trustee as trustee.

The United Kingdom

For those who are not resident or domiciled in England, Scotland or Northern Ireland, the United Kingdom offers tax haven facilities, notably that of the non-resident company. London has been historically a centre of international business, and, despite the country's other economic problems, the financial and other service industries in the capital have retained their international standing. There is no exchange control, and the Act of Parliament which authorised the Regulations in force until 1979 has been repealed. The client who uses the United Kingdom will find a level of expertise—in law, accounting, investment and administration—which he is unlikely to encounter elsewhere in the tax haven world, and at a price which compares favourably with the costs of doing business in other jurisdictions. A small company can be formed for $500; "off-the-shelf" companies are available. There is, however, one important drawback: the United Kingdom is a highly-taxed country (though not, by international standards, so highly taxed as the inhabitants generally believe), and it has a mass of sophisticated—not to say over-complicated—legislation for assessing and collecting tax. While it is possible for non-resident and non-domiciled people to base offshore operations in the United Kingdom without exposure to any local tax—and large numbers of them presently do so, there are pitfalls on every side, and the client who uses the United Kingdom must be prepared not only to take professional advice but to follow it carefully.

The principles on which a "non-resident U.K. company" functions as a zero-tax vehicle are easily stated. The United Kingdom does not tax companies by reference to their place of incorporation. A company is liable to U.K. tax on its worldwide income if—and only if—it is resident in the United Kingdom, and it is treated as resident there if it is "managed and controlled" there. In the ordinary case, it is managed and controlled where the members of the board hold their meetings. These must be real and meaningful meetings: if meetings are held in country A which merely rubber-stamp decisions taken in country B, then the true management and control is in country B, and that is where the company is resident. This concept of taxation by reference to residence is incorporated in the laws of many British and formerly British territories. (To this generalisation, the notable exception is Hong Kong.) This taxation by reference to residence is the basis of the "corporation tax" company in Guernsey, Jersey and the Isle of Man, and non-resident companies can be incorporated in many parts of the British Commonwealth, and, so long as it can be shown that they are not resident there, they suffer no local tax on their income or gains (except such as arise in the territory concerned). This applies to several of the other jurisdictions mentioned in this book—Antigua, Barbados, British Virgin Islands, Cyprus and Gibraltar. It also applies to Grenada, Israel, Singapore, St. Vincent and Swaziland.

The United Kingdom, like most other countries, taxes the non-resident on income which arises there; exceptionally, interest on many types of government security and interests on deposits with U.K. banks are exempt from tax in the hands of non-residents. Non-residents have a wider measure of exemption from capital gains tax: a non-resident company is not liable to capital gains tax on disposals of assets situated in the United Kingdom, unless it carries on a trade in the United Kingdom through a branch or agency, when a charge arises on the disposal of U.K. assets used in the trade or held for or by the branch.

The "control" which is relevant for these purposes is the control of the directors and not that of the shareholders. Where the shareholders reside is not strictly relevant. As a practical matter, however, persons resident in the United Kingdom should not attempt to use a non-resident U.K. company: the Inland Revenue appear to have set their face against the use of non-resident U.K. companies by resident taxpayers. But where the shareholders are non-residents, the Revenue are inclined to adopt an altogether more relaxed attitude. The registered office of the company should be in London, and in one of the City or West End tax districts where the Inspector is accustomed to dealing with non-resident companies. In such a case, the Inspector will generally accept the non-resident status of the company on the basis of a statement to that effect by the accountant or lawyer acting for the company in the United Kingdom, and his enquiries will be limited to verifying, at intervals of two or three years, that the company has not changed its residence and has not had any U.K. source income. Enquiries from the Revenue are time-consuming, and the company needs to incur the cost of professional advice in order to deal with them correctly. There are therefore obvious savings to be made in ensuring that a non-resident company is established in such a way that its non-resident status is accepted by the Revenue from the beginning. As to whether or not it is necessary to reveal to the tax authorities the identity of the beneficial owners of the shares in a non-resident company, there does not seem to be a uniform practice. Sometimes the Inspector will accept the assurance of a professional firm that the beneficial owners, or, where the shares are held by trustees, the beneficiaries under the trust are all resident outside the United Kingdom, but in many cases this will not be a matter of great moment, for the U.K. Revenue have a good reputation in performing their duty of confidentiality as regards the information in their possession, though residents of countries with which the United Kingdom has a tax treaty should always bear in mind that the treaty will contain provisions for the exchange of information between the taxing authorities of the two countries.

In the great majority of cases, the non-residence of the company is agreed with the Inspector at the beginning and confirmed from time to time and no further correspondence is entered into. There is, however, always the possibility that the non-resident status of a company may be called in question at some stage, and if questions are asked by the Inland Revenue authorities, answers have to be given. In this respect, a company incorporated in the United Kingdom is at a disadvantage compared with, say, a company incorporated in Turks and Caicos. If a Turks and Caicos company does not wish to give information to the Inland Revenue, there is no way in which it can be forced to do so. By contrast, the Revenue may effectively impose penalties on a U.K. company, by assessing it to an estimated amount of tax and taking proceedings to recover the tax. A company incorporated in the United Kingdom should therefore be at all times in a position to demonstrate that its management and control is exercised outside the United Kingdom. Board meetings should be held at reasonable intervals, and the minutes of those meetings should be drafted carefully. The minutes should show that the individual who is the real "brains" of a company (if there be such a person) was present at the meeting, that matters of moment were discussed and resolved upon, and generally that the true management and control of the company was exercised in the place in which it was purported to be exercised. At the same time, any information of a politically or commercially sensitive nature, which the company would not wish to see produced before a tribunal in the United Kingdom—or, still less, appearing in a case stated in the report of an appeal to the High Court—should be studiously omitted. If there is a dispute with the Inland Revenue about the residence of a company, it is helpful—although it is not strictly necessary—for the company to be able to show that it was resident in some other jurisdiction: a "gypsy" company—one whose board meetings were held in a succession of different places—would carry less conviction with a tribunal, and for this reason the directors should aim to hold their meetings consistently in the same place. This should not, of course, be a place which itself imposes tax by reason of the holding of directors' meetings there. Hong Kong and Monaco are frequently used for this purpose, but meetings could be held in the Bahamas or some other zero-tax jurisdiction or in Gibraltar, if a company is registered there as exempt, and consideration may also be given to countries which do not have the "management and control" criterion for taxability, such as Belgium, Denmark, France, Germany, Luxembourg, the Netherlands, Panama, Switzerland or the United States.

The cost of forming a company in the United Kingdom will be about £300 (U.S.$480). "Off-the-shelf" companies are commonly used. A company may be formed in England or in Scotland or in Northern Ireland. The legal requirements are somewhat different in each case, but in every case the original constitution of the company (the "memorandum and articles") and any subsequent amendments are filed in the Companies Register, as are the names of the shareholders (though nominee names are permitted). The Register is open to public inspection. A limited company must also file its annual accounts, but a small company files only an abbreviated balance sheet and a medium-sized company an abbreviated balance sheet and profit and loss account. If the amount of financial information to be made available to the public is unacceptable to the intending shareholders, they may wish instead to consider forming an unlimited company. Such a company does not have the word "Limited" in its name. It does not, of course, offer the shareholders the benefits of limited liability, but this problem may be overcome by causing the shares to be held by limited companies incorporated elsewhere. A minimum of two registered shareholders is required, so that this solution requires two limited companies incorporated elsewhere, for although it is possible in theory for the two shares to be held by nominees or trustees, it is unlikely in practice that nominees or trustees can be found who will be willing to hold shares in an unlimited company.

The company must maintain a "registered office" in the United Kingdom and state the address on its writing paper. Any legal proceedings would be served on the company at this address, and it is this address which determines in what tax district the company's affairs are dealt with. A form of bearer share is available, called the "share warrant to bearer." The company cannot have shares of no par value, but the par value of the shares does not have to be expressed in sterling. The company may redeem its ordinary shares out of profits. The minimum number of shareholders is two, either or both of whom may be nominees. There must be at least one director and a secretary (though a sole director may not also be the secretary), and it is not requisite that any of the officers of the company be resident in the United Kingdom. The *ultra vires* rule is still, in a modified form, in force in the United Kingdom, and it is therefore the practice for the objects of the company to be drawn in a wide form. A shareholders' meeting (the Annual General Meeting) must be held once a year. Government approval is required for the establishment of a bank or insurance company, but a trust company may be formed without the necessity of any kind of licence. Incorporation costs are low, but the United Kingdom, following the practice in other EEC countries, imposes a 1 per cent. capital duty on the issue of shares in limited companies (but not on the issue of shares in unlimited companies). The accounts to be filed must be audited accounts, and the cost of auditing must be taken into account in assessing the costs of maintaining a non-resident company in the United Kingdom.

A feature of the U.K. tax system which represents perhaps the most serious pitfall for the investor in a U.K. non-resident company is the existence of inheritance tax. This is a combination of a gift tax and an estate tax; though certain gifts now fall outside the ambit of the tax, the death of a shareholder, and certain other events, may be an occasion of a charge to tax, even though the shareholder is resident and domiciled outside the United Kingdom. These problems are generally circumvented by the interposition of an offshore company between the shareholder and the U.K. company. Thus, for example, if the shareholder lives in Italy, he might form an IBC in the British Virgin Islands, which in turn holds the shares of an English non-resident company; the assets which would pass on his death are not the shares in the English company but the shares in the BVI company. Individuals domiciled outside the United Kingdom are only liable to inheritance tax on assets situated in the United Kingdom. Shares in a company incorporated in any part of the United Kingdom are situated in the United Kingdom for these purposes. In the example, the Italian, having interposed an IBC between himself and his English company, would die possessed of assets situated in the British Virgin Islands (which has no inheritance tax or its equivalent) and not possessed of any assets situated in the United Kingdom.

England is the original home of the trust, and the trust corporation, acting as a professional trustee for a large number of trusts, is an important and well-established part of the financial services industry in the United Kingdom. Parliament seems to have gone out of its way, when enacting taxing legislation, to ensure that individuals who are not resident or domiciled in the United Kingdom will be encouraged to make use of these services when establishing a trust, or at any rate not be wholly discouraged from doing so by the nature of the U.K. tax system. The result is a rather messy mixture of chargeability and exemption but the U.K. trust can be a very attractive option in a number of special circumstances (and for a consideration of such special circumstances the reader may refer to the author's *The World of International Tax Planning*, Cambridge University Press, 1984): there are even circumstances where a settlor can obtain for his trust the benefit of a tax treaty to which the United Kingdom is a party, even though the trust has no exposure to United Kingdom tax. But this book is concerned with tax planning opportunities of a general nature, and here one is basically looking at two kinds of trusts established in the United Kingdom—those which have foreign income payable to non-resident beneficiaries, and those which have no income at all but from time to time have capital gains.

The general rule is that a trustee resident in the United Kingdom is liable to pay tax on trust income, whether it is distributed or not. However, where the trustee is a bare trustee—that is, the trustee holds the assets as a pure nominee for the beneficial owner, or where there is a beneficiary who is entitled to the trust income as it arises (typically the "life tenant," who enjoys the trust income during his lifetime), and (a) the trust income arises outside the United Kingdom and (b) the person entitled to the income resides outside the United Kingdom, the trust is treated as transparent for income tax purposes, and no liability for income tax arises.

Where the trust assets consist of shares in one or more underlying companies which declare no dividends, no question of income tax of course arises. In both such cases—the "transparent" trust and the incomeless trust—the United Kingdom will have advantages comparable to those of other territories in this book only if the trust assets are free from capital gains tax and inheritance tax. Fortunately, this is generally speaking so. As far as capital gains tax is concerned, so long as the settlor is neither resident, ordinarily resident nor domiciled in the United Kingdom, and so long as the trustee (generally a trust corporation) is a "professional" trustee—that is, one who is carrying on business as such, then the trustee will be treated, as regards the trust assets, as not resident in the United Kingdom, and will be free of capital gains tax accordingly. For inheritance tax purposes, the beneficiary entitled to the income under a "transparent" trust is treated as the owner for the time being of the trust assets, so that if the beneficiary is not domiciled in the United Kingdom and the trust assets are situated outside the United Kingdom, there will be no liability to inheritance tax. A similar exemption from inheritance tax is conferred upon the foreign assets of other trusts, so long as the settlor was domiciled outside the United Kingdom when he settled the assets.

Vanuatu

The Republic of Vanuatu was formerly the Anglo-French condominium of the New Hebrides. It consists of 80 islands, of which several are uninhabited, scattered over a large area of the South Pacific, some 1,500 miles north-east of Sydney. It has no income tax or other direct taxation, and it offers zero-tax companies of the English type. The law applicable to commerce and trusts is basically English. English and French are official languages and the languages of commerce; a form of pidgin English called Bislama is the lingua franca and widely used.

For offshore activities the company limited by shares is generally used. It may, and generally will be, an "exempt" company. *Exempt* does not here imply any exemption from tax (of which there is none) or from restrictions on foreign ownership of shares, nor is any government guarantee given against any future taxes. An exempt company benefits from the secrecy regulations: all information filed with the Registrar is confidential and any improper disclosure of this information is punishable by law. A minimum of two subscribers is required, and particulars of the beneficial owners are not supplied to Government but may be required by the trust company undertaking the incorporation. Shares in a private exempt company may be of no par value or have a par value, and they may be in registered or bearer form. The name of the company must end in the word "Limited."

Every company needs to have a local director and a secretary. Other directors may be of any nationality or residence. The local trust company responsible for the incorporation and maintenance of the company may supply all the directors and give certain limited powers to others to act on behalf of the company. Alternatively, the trust company supplies one local director, who is joined by one or more directors resident abroad, but in that case the trust company monitors the activities of the company and if it does not approve is in a position, as a last resort, to cause the company to be struck off the register. Every tax haven has to face, one way or the other, the problem of balancing its desire to give secrecy and freedom of action to the client with its need to preserve the good name of the jurisdiction. The solution adopted in Vanuatu is vetting by the trust company coupled with stringent secrecy rules.

Private exempt companies (other than banks, trust companies and insurance companies), require no audit. Foreign companies may be redomiciled in Vanuatu, and local companies continued elsewhere. A bank, trust company or insurance company also requires a licence, but banks and insurance companies conducting offshore business only are free of the various reporting duties which must be observed by local insurance companies and banks. The cost of an offshore banking licence is U.S.$3,000 a year and an insurance company licence U.S.$1,000.

The cost of incorporating an ordinary exempt company in Vanuatu is of the order of U.S.$1,000, and a similar annual fee covers maintenance costs.